How to Build an Instructional

COACHING
PROGRAM

for

Maximum
Capacity

*We would like to dedicate this book in memory
and honor of our first coaches, our parents—*

Dr. and Mrs. Franklin B. Jones

Dr. and Mrs. Fred G. Staton

The gift of their enduring love and support is immeasurable.

How to Build an Instructional

COACHING PROGRAM

for

Maximum

Capacity

Nina Jones Morel
Carla Staton Cushman
Foreword by Stephen G. Barkley

CORWIN
A SAGE Company

CORWIN
A SAGE Company

FOR INFORMATION:

Corwin
A SAGE Company
2455 Teller Road
Thousand Oaks, California 91320
(800) 233-9936
www.corwin.com

SAGE Publications Ltd.
1 Oliver's Yard
55 City Road
London EC1Y 1SP
United Kingdom

SAGE Publications India Pvt. Ltd.
B 1/I 1 Mohan Cooperative Industrial Area
Mathura Road, New Delhi 110 044
India

SAGE Publications Asia-Pacific Pte. Ltd.
3 Church Street
#10-04 Samsung Hub
Singapore 049483

Acquisitions Editor: Dan Alpert
Associate Editor: Megan Bedell
Editorial Assistant: Sarah Bartlett
Permissions Editor: Karen Ehrmann
Project Editor: Veronica Stapleton
Copy Editor: Kim Husband
Typesetter: C&M Digitals (P) Ltd.
Proofreader: Wendy Jo Dymond
Indexer: Jean Casalegno
Cover Designer: Karine Hovsepian

Interior photographs by David L. Morel.

Printed in the United States of America.

Library of Congress Cataloging-in-Publication Data

Morel, Nina.

How to build an instructional coaching program for maximum capacity / Nina Morel, Carla Cushman. Foreword by Stephen G. Barkley.

p. cm.
Includes bibliographical references and index.

ISBN 978-1-4522-0289-1 (pbk.)

1. Teachers—In-service training. 2. Professional learning communities. 3. School improvement programs. I. Cushman, Carla. II. Title.

LB1731.M65 2012
370.71'1—dc23   2011045936

This book is printed on acid-free paper.

MIX
Paper from
responsible sources
FSC® C014174
www.fsc.org

12 13 14 15 16 10 9 8 7 6 5 4 3 2 1

Contents

Foreword   viii
Stephen G. Barkley

Acknowledgments   xi

About the Authors   xiii

Chapter 1 Prevailing Winds:
   Navigating the Perfect Storm   1

   Boarding the Ship   4
   Consulting the Compass: Convincing the Mind   6
   Feeling the Wind in Your Hair: Convincing the Heart   8
   Sailing With the Current: Structuring the Practice   9
   Following North Stars: Understanding Coaching Basics   10
   Bon Voyage   11

Chapter 2 Dead Reckoning:
   Beginning With the End in Mind   13

   Let Go of Certainty   14
   Clarify Your Vision   15
   Figure Your Present Location   17
   Strengthen or Abandon   18
   Determine How Far You Have to Go   19
   Move From Vision to Plan   20
   Summary   28

Chapter 3 Sounding the Depths:
   Using Data for Reflecting, Refining, and Celebrating   31

   Identify Program Goals and Coaching Goals   32
   Determine Your Purpose   33

Determine the Measures to Meet
    Your Purposes and Goals 36
Be Prepared to Face the Challenges and the Treasures 37
Determine What Kinds of Data You Will Collect 38
Evaluate and Communicate the Results 43
Share Assessment Results With Coaches,
    Teachers, or Administrators 44
Celebrate Success 46
Summary 47

Chapter 4 Ready, Set, Sail: Selecting the Coaching Crew **49**

Apply Your Coaching Administrative Model
    to Your Hiring Plan 50
Know What You Want in a Coach 54
Summary: Wrapping Up the Hiring Process 63

Chapter 5 O, Captain, My Captain:
Preparing the Principal **65**

Preparing Principals for Instructional Coaching 66
Leading a Change Initiative 66
How Instructional Coaching Supports and
    Facilitates Change 68
The Role of the Instructional Coach 68
The Role of the Principal 70
The Role of the Coaching Champion 72
Communication Among Stakeholders 72
The Principal–Coach Memorandum of Understanding 74
Voices From the Field 74
A Sample Plan for Preparing Principals for Coaching 75
Summary 76

Chapter 6 Anchors Aweigh: Preparing Coaches
Through Preservice Instruction **79**

Prioritize Specific Knowledge and
    Skill Sets to Deepen and Refine 80
Develop a Preservice Instructional Plan 81
Don't Forget the Captain! 86
Summary 88

Chapter 7 All Hands on Deck:
Preparing the Teachers and Staff **91**

Smooth Sailing or Rough Seas? 92
Start With the Best 93

Develop Mini-Champions 94

Connect Coaching to One's School and Personal Vision 96

Accept Resistance 97

Hone the Message 97

Use Sticky Ideas 98

Tell a Story, Be a Part of a Story 99

Know Your Goal: A Culture of Collegiality 101

Provide the Appropriate Environment for Coaching 103

Perfect Storms 106

Summary 106

Chapter 8 Trimming the Sails:
Ongoing Professional Learning and Support 109

Friday Focus and Sí C-C 110

Consultants 111

Technology Training 112

Coach the Coach 113

Conferences 113

Site Visits 114

Coaching Academy Partnership 114

Relationship 116

Summary 117

Chapter 9 Mooring the Ship: Avalon or Ithaca? 119

Study and Respond to Your Results 121

Expand Your Program 122

Sustain Your Program 123

Change Your Program 124

Abandon and Reimagine 127

Actualize 127

Resources 128

References 167

Facilitator's Guide 171

References for Facilitator's Guide 202

Index 204

Foreword

A few years ago, Carla Cushman and Nina Morel called to tell me they had been charged with designing and implementing an instructional coaching program in Tennessee's Sumner County schools. I was delighted, as I first met these school leaders during a training session I held on instructional coaching at a Reading Summit in Tennessee. Carla and Nina were new to coaching then and purchased my book *Quality Teaching in a Culture of Coaching*®.

Early in our subsequent conversation, Carla and Nina asked me to recommend a book that would guide them through the actual process of creating such a program, from the envisioning stage to designing to planning. They wanted to gain ideas about the appropriate professional training that might be required and how to launch and implement the program. In my *Quality Teaching in a Culture of Coaching*® book, I stress the value and importance of creating a coaching culture in schools, but I had to be honest with them—I did not know of a book that specifically guided the process of creating and implementing a program within a school jurisdiction.

So they decided to write the book themselves, even though, as they both admitted, they did not have a lot of direct experience with coaching prior to receiving their assignment. That changed quickly as they delved into research and the study of coaching skills and strategies. They flew out to Salem, Oregon, where I was holding a week-long instructional coaching training and interviewed me and others on the process. Bringing what they learned back to Tennessee, they practiced in the roles of coach and coachee. Nina and Carla became immersed in coaching as they shadowed other coaches, teachers, and administrators, testing theories and gleaning ideas from their experiences as well as creating ideas of their own.

Their book is a culmination of this knowledge and practice of instructional coaching along with their own now more substantial experiences within the world of coaching. Carla and Nina guide the reader through the process of creating an effective instructional coaching program and touch on all the aspects in a step-by-step, chapter-by-chapter approach while weaving a delightful metaphor of navigating a ship through waters rough and calm.

The book will find its way to central office and building administrators looking to start or refine a coaching program. School board members and others studying school leadership will achieve great insights not only into creating a viable coaching plan but also in learning a model that offers ways to improve their existing programs. The authors' efforts and research underscore their point that they are promoting not just a coaching program but an overall culture of collaboration and professional learning. Central to the theme embedded within the process is the importance of teachers moving from isolation to collaboration, with principals and instructional coaches supporting them along the way.

As we pointed out in *Instructional Coaching With the End in Mind: Using Backwards Planning to Increase Student Achievement*, teaching is a complex profession, compounded by the day. Time and again, research has borne out the tremendous value of coaching. It offers support and refines teaching methods that enhance teaching and student learning alike. An instructional coach performs a balanced act between principal and teacher. A skilled instructional coach can spell the difference between an enthusiastic faculty with proactive professional development programs and engaged student population and those schools or districts that scramble to keep up with teaching mandates and parent demands.

In this book, Carla and Nina sketch out a navigational guide for a journey toward an effective instructional coaching program. It is not necessarily a destination. As the authors point out, just as the use of cell phones has become a part of our way of life, coaching in many districts has become an integral part of their culture. At the same time, coaching may not change a culture so much as the culture influences the coaching program, so that instructional coaches become quasisupervisors or assistant principals. Each school, each district, each teacher, principal, and instructional coach will encounter different successes and challenges. The thrust, however, is to change the tradition of teaching in isolation to one of collaboration and teamwork, sharing and transparency, where the engagement of students always remains the end goal.

This is a significant book that provides guidance in the aspects of instructional coaching programs. It describes methods to present the concept, create or elicit the vision; it outlines characteristics to look for when hiring an instructional coach; the importance of communicating to stakeholders; how to enroll and gain buy-in from principals; what training and support are needed; and what to do with resistance and challenges—what they cleverly refer to as "squalls."

Chapter 7 in particular provides motivation and answers the unasked questions about who gets coached first and why, how the process works and in what environment, and how to tell the story that drives the desire to take the risks and reap the rewards of a coaching culture destined to improve and augment the value of teachers, coaches, principals, and students alike.

In the event readers are not sure where to begin their journeys, a Facilitator's Guide to follow or adapt as desired provides a real "anchor" for this navigational guide.

Carla and Nina do not have all the answers for you. But they do have the questions that will lead you to design an instructional coaching program of your own. Just as an effective instructional coach develops a teacher's capacity to reflect and create and experiment in an ongoing continuous improvement cycle, so too does *How to Build an Instructional Coaching Program for Maximum Capacity* coach you on a journey to create a program with stellar results.

Thank you, Carla and Nina, for your remarkable contribution to building a culture of coaching.

Stephen G. Barkley
Executive Vice President
Performance Learning Systems, Inc.
Author, Quality Teaching in a Culture of Coaching® *and*
Instructional Coaching With the End in Mind:
Using Backwards Planning to Increase Student Achievement

Acknowledgments

The authors wish to acknowledge their friends and colleagues in Sumner County, Tennessee, who contributed their wisdom, patience, energy, and heart in pursuit of the development of an exemplary instructional coaching program. We especially wish to acknowledge the vision of Judy Wheeler, who gave us the opportunity to embark on this voyage. Thank you to all the coaches who have shown us what it means to exhibit *arête*. We also owe a debt of gratitude to Stephen Barkley, coach of coaches, who coached us as fledgling coaching champions. Thank you to our students over the last 25 years, because we have learned more from them than they could possibly have learned from us.

Most of all, however, we appreciate our husbands, who have never doubted us, and our children and grandchildren, who keep teaching us about the important things in life.

Publisher's Acknowledgments

Corwin gratefully acknowledges the contributions of the following reviewers:

Kathy Cheval, Mathematics Specialist
Salem Keizer Public Schools
Salem, OR

Gail A. Epps, Program Manager
New Teacher Induction, Montgomery County Public Schools
Rockville, MD

Gregory MacDougall, Specialist
S²MART Centers
Aiken, SC

Patricia Mathues, Supervisor of Elementary Language Arts
Souderton Area School District
Souderton, PA

Rob Moyer, Professional
  Development Coordinator
  and Teacher
Perkiomen Valley School
  District
Collegeville, PA

Vanessa Nieto-Gomez,
  Training and Professional
  Development
  Administrator
Houston Independent School
  District
Houston, TX

Fernando Nunez,
  Director of Professional
  Development
Isaac School District #5
Phoenix, AZ

Rena M. Rockwell, Director
  of Professional
  Development
Ritenour School District
St. Louis, MO

Debi Rozeski,
  Coordinator
  of Professional
  Development
Moreno Valley Unified
  School District
Moreno Valley, CA

Lloyd Sain, Director,
  Leadership and Secondary
  Teacher Development
Little Rock School District
Little Rock, AR

Elizabeth Sandall, Staff
  Development Content
  Specialist for Middle School
  Instruction
Montgomery County Public
  Schools
Rockville, MD

Bradley Schleder, District
  Academic Coach, Science
Kings Canyon Unified School
  District
Reedley, CA

Lewis E. Stonaker, Jr., Staff
  Development Coordinator/
  Educational Consultant
Monroe Township Public
  Schools/Personalized
  Professional Development,
  LLC
Robbinsville, NJ

Deb Wallace, Instructional
  Specialist and Professional
  Developer
iCoaching Team
S^{2}TEM Centers
Clemson, SC

About the Authors

Nina Jones Morel, EdD, is an associate professor of education and director of master's programs at Lipscomb University in Nashville, Tennessee. She was a 2005 winner of the Milken Foundation National Educator Award and has taught at the middle, high school, undergraduate, and graduate levels. She has served as a school district administrator and a coaching champion. She is married and has three adult children and two stepchildren.

Carla Staton Cushman, EdS, is the director of the Sumner County Teacher Center in Gallatin, Tennessee, and a coaching champion. She began her career in education as an elementary teacher and has served as a middle school assistant principal and principal. She is currently a doctoral candidate at Union University in Hendersonville, Tennessee. Carla is married and has two adult children and four grandchildren.

Building an Instructional Coaching Program for Maximum Capacity

1. Research coaching and coaching models. Reach out to others (coaches, coaching champions) in the professional community. (Chapter 1)

2. Select a "champion team" who will develop the coaching initiative and will support coaching. (Chapter 2)

3. Develop a shared vision of instructional coaching for your school or district. (Chapter 2)

4. Align your vision of instructional coaching with your school or district's vision. (Chapter 2)

5. Develop an administrative model for coaching. (Chapter 2)

6. Develop your assessment plan for the coaching initiative. Know what you will evaluate and how you will do it. (Chapter 3)

7. Know the five characteristics of great coaches prior to hiring and assigning, and use them to develop a recruitment strategy. Interview and hire coaches. (Chapter 4)

8. Determine preservice training needs for administrators and supervisors and develop a learning plan. (Chapter 5)

9. Determine preservice training needs for newly hired instructional coaches and develop a learning plan for the first of the school year as part of a long-term comprehensive model of ongoing professional learning and support. (Chapter 6)

10. Plan for opportunities for regular collaboration among and between coaches and teachers after coaches begin. (Chapter 7)

11. Develop a model of ongoing learning and support for instructional coaches. (Chapter 8)

12. Evaluate your coaching program and make necessary adjustments to sustain, change, abandon, or reimagine your coaching initiative. (Chapters 3 and 9)

1

Prevailing Winds

Navigating the Perfect Storm

If you are reading this book, you are probably a leader who is already interested in the potential of coaching. Perhaps you are an administrator for a school or district that is considering implementation of an instructional coaching program, or maybe you are an educator who is preparing to be an administrator. You might even be a teacher leader who recognizes a need in your own school and wants to learn what might be involved in starting a coaching program. Perhaps you were intrigued when you saw the benefits firsthand in another school or district—or perhaps, like us, you have been asked to start a coaching program and you do not really know how to begin. This book is a navigational guide for you as you embark on your coaching voyage.

Over the course of our careers, we have weathered a lot of storms, from the *Nation at Risk* (1983) to No Child Left Behind (2001). Despite these programs' impact, most people would agree that what was actually happening in most American classrooms was little changed from what it was in 1975. But in recent years, many educational, social, and economic realities have come together in the "perfect storm" that is now transforming public and political attitudes toward schooling in America. In many states, standards are higher, tests are harder, and teacher and principal evaluations are including individual and school value-added statistics. Teachers are called upon to exhibit expertise in their content, the standards, pedagogy, assessment, statistics, and diverse cultures and learning styles. The very concept of *public school* is being reimagined. All of this is in the context of intense economic pressure in a "flattening" world where globalization is forcing greater and greater economic competition with the world's largest countries of India and China (Friedman, 2005). In this maelstrom of change, it is finally becoming apparent to American schools what other countries such as Finland, South Korea, and Singapore have embraced for some time: Sustained and embedded support for collaboration, action research, and peer observation must occur in order for teachers and learning organizations to reach their potential (Darling-Hammond, 2010–2011). We think of this as maximum capacity.

Fullan (2008) states that "individuals and groups are high in capacity if they possess and continue to develop knowledge and skills, if they attract and use resources . . . wisely, and if they are committed to putting in the energy to get important things done *collectively* and *continuously*" (p. 57). It seems that the sociocultural learning theory formulated by Vygotsky (1978) and others is as applicable to the professional learning of teachers as to the educational learning of children. The way to maximize the capacity of teachers to meet student needs is to embed professional learning in the cultural and social life of the school. No one person can navigate the complexities of modern educational reality alone behind closed classroom doors or sitting in a lecture hall listening to experts. This new climate requires continuously improved teacher knowledge, skills, effectiveness, and collaboration embedded within the daily work lives of teachers. There are different methods to accomplish this goal, but this book is about the way that we found worked best for our learning organization—instructional coaching—and ways to implement it in any school.

> According to the U.S. Department of Education website (2009), "Doing What Works," one of the keys to education reform is improving teacher effectiveness . . . and strategies to do that include redesigning staff learning to ensure it is "sustained, job-embedded, collaborative, data-driven, and focused on student instructional needs."

Over the years, as teachers and then as administrators, the authors came to believe that effective professional learning must take place in the context of the particular work situation of the teacher. Some schools in our district had great success with the professional learning community (PLC) model of professional growth, and this experience heightened our desire for deeper and richer professional dialog for all of our teachers. Like most districts, the majority of our meager professional learning dollars were spent bringing in professional presenters to provide instruction in workshop-type settings. We always knew that when the opportunity arose, we would take a different path. And indeed, the resources came, and we and our colleagues were asked to create a coaching program in our district in a very short time frame.

We began by researching the literature on coaching models and implementation recommendations. We found many sources that helped us narrow our focus to the one approach to coaching we felt matched our needs and vision. However, the book we kept looking for was a step-by-step guide to take us from the dream to the reality, and we could not find it. Most of the books we read were very helpful for our coaches, but they were not practical guides for large-scale implementation. There were many excellent resources for one to acquire deep knowledge about the various forms of coaching and the strategies coaches employ, but no plan of attack for two newly appointed and inexperienced coaching facilitators who had about 2 months to develop a program and then hire, train, and deploy a cadre of instructional coaches to make a difference in student achievement. This book can be that guide for you.

When we were faced with the challenge of starting a coaching program, not only were we untrained as coaches ourselves, but we had never even been formally coached in any setting other than athletics. Although coaching had become ubiquitous in the realms of counseling and business, in the pre-K–12 world in which we operated, it had only been the rare and well-funded district that believed it could afford instructional or academic coaches on any large scale. This meant we were asked to implement a change initiative with very little personal knowledge or experience and to help teachers and administrators understand what coaching is and why implementing a coaching program is a better solution to school-improvement issues than are other options, such as lower class size, increased technology purchases, or adding more support personnel.

Our first step was to assess our own strengths and challenges as leaders. Although we knew little about coaching, we both had education and experience in implementing change initiatives. We also had the advantage of knowing our personnel: We had some understanding of the needs, motivation, background, and vision of our district, teachers, and principals. We determined to use these assets to build our project, and we embarked on a learning process about coaching, the missing link in our knowledge base. To compensate for our gaps in knowledge, we sought out experts and practitioners in the field by reading their work and, in some cases, by contacting them personally and asking for advice.

You may be in a different situation. You may be new to your position and know a lot about coaching and little about your school or district. You may be very familiar with coaching and know your personnel well but know little about implementing large-scale change. Your first step is taking an honest look at what your strengths and challenges are and making a research plan based on those. This book does not attempt to teach you everything you need to know about coaching, leadership, or change, and it certainly cannot teach you about your own school or district culture, personnel, and vision, but hopefully it will give you a framework on which to place your own leadership skills and knowledge as you develop a successful coaching initiative.

Boarding the Ship

When the two of us initially discussed writing a book about our experience with coaching, one of the first images that came to our minds was Homer's *Odyssey*. When we began implementing the coaching initiative, we felt like we were embarking on a long voyage that might have lots of exciting and sometimes harrowing adventures. What we were planning for was (in some cases) a drastic change in school culture. How we approached that change would have a great impact on whether the experience would lead to growth or chaos. We needed a clear vision, a detailed plan, and ways to motivate others to embrace change. With that, we felt, we could handle whatever Cyclops came our way.

Schmoker (2006) argues that school and district cultures have created a protective buffer for America's classrooms by granting almost complete autonomy to teachers. Administrators have left teachers to themselves, rarely monitoring and supervising their instructional practices. Teachers have been isolated, withholding best practices from each other and experiencing very few professional collaborative experiences. While this isolation can be crippling to growth, it was what most of our teachers knew, and it seemed less intimidating than engaging in teaching as a public act. Our challenge was not to learn what teachers should do in classrooms—there is ample research indicating good instructional practices—but to make sure teachers could make those practices happen in the classroom. We wanted to make teaching a team endeavor, something that has eluded reformers for 50 years. Could instructional coaching be the answer?

In short, we had to cast off from the familiarity and safety of our so-called *Isolation Islands* and sail toward a collaborative culture where educators grasp the vital link between professional learning and student learning. We believe instructional coaches can help teachers (and principals!) maximize their individual and collective capacities by championing collaborative practices. However, coaching can banish isolation only if coaching becomes a part of the culture *and* changes the culture. In a brief few years, cellular technology has become both a part of our culture and has changed our culture. Looking back, isn't it hard to believe we all led perfectly full, productive, and happy lives without cell phones? Yet when they were first introduced, we remember people exclaiming, "I would never have one of those things! What a nuisance!" In many places, coaches impact the culture like cell phones. People stop their coaches in the hall and say, "How did we ever get along without you!" In other schools and districts, this is not the case. Instead of the culture being changed, the culture ends up changing the coaching. Sometimes coaches become de facto supervisors or assistant principals. In other situations, the coach becomes a general "dogsbody" (in the Royal Navy slang)—someone who does the work no one else wants to do. What makes the difference in coaching programs that change the culture and those that do not? To find the answer, we turned to theories of change implementation and tried to apply them to our situation.

For effective change to take place, people have to change their minds, emotions, and practices. Chip and Dan Heath's book on this topic, *Switch* (2010), provides a compelling picture: Change is like a man riding an elephant down a path. You have to direct the rider (mind), motivate the elephant (emotion), and shape the path (systems and procedures) to get to the destination. To a leader starting a coaching initiative, this means that providing a clear vision and information that shows how and why coaching works is important, but only part of the process. You must also motivate people to have an emotional need to change and you must set up the processes that make the change as easy as possible. To translate Heath and Heath's ideas into our nautical metaphor, the sailor has to consult the compass, feel the wind in his or her hair, and sail with the current.

Consulting the Compass: Convincing the Mind

When starting any journey, we want to make sure we're going in the right direction. The same is true when we implement a new initiative, perhaps even more so because of the inherent responsibility we have for all those who follow our lead. So how do you know that coaching will move your own school or district in the right direction, and what evidence do you give others of that? Instructional coaching is a professional learning model, so we turned to Learning Forward (formerly the National Staff Development Council). Learning Forward defines professional learning as "a comprehensive, sustained, intensive and collaborative approach to improving teachers' and principals' effectiveness in raising student achievement." The definition goes on to state that "to ensure that effective teaching spreads, districts and schools must create professional learning systems in which teams of teachers, principals, and other professional staff members meet several times a week to engage in a continuous cycle of improvement" (Learning Forward, 2011, p. i).

In a 2003 report, Neufeld and Roper stated,

> There is reason to think that coaching, thoughtfully developed and implemented within a district's coherent professional development plan, will provide teachers with real opportunities to improve their instruction, principals with real opportunities to improve their leadership, and districts with real opportunities to improve their schools. (p. 26)

Their assertions are supported by research that shows that the most effective professional learning is "sustained and intensive"

(Darling-Hammond & Richardson, 2009). Although this could be accomplished in several models, we believed the research supported coaching as an excellent vehicle to create these professional learning systems.

As a school leader implementing coaching in your learning organization, you will want to become very familiar with the literature on coaching, a body of literature that has expanded exponentially in recent years. In addition, we recommend you explore the resources available on the Learning Forward website and other online resources specific to coaching, many of which are sponsored or hosted by coaching experts and practitioners. It is also helpful to seek out school districts and schools in which instructional coaching is already established. We have found that most educators are eager to talk about their experiences with coaching. For now, here is a summary of the rational reasons for coaching you may want to share with your school or district as you help them start their coaching journey:

1. Student achievement is the goal.

2. More effective teachers lead to greater student achievement.

3. Systems of sustained and intensive professional learning lead to more thoughtful and effective teaching practices.

4. Coaching is part of one model that can help move a school toward a system of professional learning.

5. Coaching leads to far greater implementation of strategies learned in workshop settings.

6. Teachers reap many additional professional benefits from coaching, such as greater job satisfaction and confidence in their teaching skills.

This information is not enough to close the knowing–doing gap. When implementing change in an educational organization, the research is just the beginning. The leader must communicate a clear focus and goals that seem reasonable and attainable and motivate people to take the first steps in the right direction. You don't have to know every step you will take in the middle, but a clear view of the beginning and destination is vital. Your organization's mission and vision will point you in the right direction, but it is up to you as the leader to align your coaching program with that vision and communicate how your first steps will lead your organization toward its goals.

> "When you're at the beginning, don't obsess about the middle, because the middle is going to look different once you get there. Just look for a strong beginning and a strong ending and get moving."
>
> —Chip Heath and Dan Heath (2010, p. 93)

Feeling the Wind in Your Hair: Convincing the Heart

There are strong emotional reasons to embrace coaching, and your job as a leader is to make these vivid. Teachers, principals, school staff, and community need to see clearly that coaching is for their own children's achievement. They also need to shift their mental model of a professional teacher as an *expert* to a mental model of a professional teacher as a *learning facilitator* and *collaborator*. Professional staff must embrace this as part of their emotional identity, and others must see them in this way.

Emotional benefits from coaching are extensive, and when teachers begin to experience them, your coaching program will begin to thrive. Teachers can feel lonely and isolated, especially in the early years of their careers. As Barth (2003) wrote, "our lives are a trail of un-had conversations" (p. 4). Conversations with other professionals are limited by time, schedules, and sometimes even competition. Coaching can create the delightful synergy of two professionals working together to solve problems. It can help make a school really feel like a team and can promote shared accountability and celebration.

According to Pink (2009), autonomy, mastery, and purpose are what people need to motivate them, to get them into the "flow." Coaching supports all three. It provides autonomy by allowing teachers to choose their own professional learning needs, mastery by providing a safe place to practice and improve with scaffolded support, and purpose to know that all they do is contributing to the team, which is in turn improving student learning. This doesn't mean other needs such as adequate pay and working conditions are unnecessary—but many teachers report that coaching is what put the joy back in their professional lives. Knight, in his introduction to *Instructional Coaching: A Partnership Approach to Improving Instruction* (2007), wrote, "When people talk about learning, the experience should be exciting, energizing, and empowering" (p. ix). Barkley, in his aptly named book, *Quality Teaching in a Culture of Coaching* (2010), states it simply: "It feels good to improve, to change, and to succeed; it feels good to have someone in your corner, coaching you to high achievement" (p. 11).

Sailing With the Current: Structuring the Practice

Finally, and perhaps most exhaustingly, your job of developing a coaching program will require setting up systems and procedures in the environment (the path) that make the journey to a coaching culture easy. If you are a district administrator, you have several paths to forge—for your building administrators, your coaches, and your teachers. Each will require time, processes, and resources.

The goal of this book is to provide you with the tools to create an organizational structure for building a successful coaching initiative. The essential components of that structure are discussed in each of the chapters that follow. In **Chapter 2,** you will align your coaching program with the mission, vision, and goals of your school or district and answer some basic questions about your program's structure. In **Chapter 3,** you will determine how you will collect and use data to reflect, refine, and celebrate your coaching program. In **Chapter 4,** you will examine six characteristics of great coaches and strategies to discern them in the hiring process. You will plan preservice learning for school administrators in **Chapter 5** and preservice learning for newly hired coaches in **Chapter 6. Chapter 7** will take you to the heart of coaching as you create ways to motivate teachers and staff to take the first steps into a more collaborative culture. Regardless of how many years the newly appointed instructional coach may have taught in the classroom, transitioning to the role of instructional coach will require navigating unfamiliar and sometimes unchartered waters. In **Chapter 8,** you will develop a successful model of ongoing professional learning and support to help your fledgling and developing coaches. At the end of one cycle of implementation, the next cycle begins—reevaluation, realignment, and reimplementation. In **Chapter 9,** you will discover practical ways to monitor and sustain your coaching program in light of unforeseen promise and possibilities of the future. To help you on your journey, the **Resources** section includes sample forms to assist you in setting up and administering a coaching program from the planning and hiring process to the program evaluation stage.

We have also included a comprehensive **Facilitator's Guide** to use with your own small study group or professional learning community. The guide contains music, metaphors, and guiding questions to engage participants in reflective thought and dialogue for practical application to your school or district goals. Good teachers provide hundreds of mental hooks for students to connect information to prior knowledge or emotion—music, story, song, metaphor, humor.

We want our work to provide lots of hooks for you to connect the information, and we also want to provide you with a model that you can use in sharing this information with your colleagues.

Gardner (2006) asserts that telling stories is one of the most effective ways to change people's minds, whether we're telling stories to someone who is very close to us or someone who hardly knows us. We believe in the power of story and use many applicable stories and scenarios. In a broader sense, however, the book itself is a story of a journey, with inspiration from the great tradition of sea stories, plays, and songs. The metaphor of a sea journey is one of the strongest in Western literature and gives a narrative structure to the text that will make it easier to remember and, hopefully, to share.

Following North Stars: Understanding Coaching Basics

As stated in the introduction to this chapter, the intent of this book is not to explain and describe what coaching is; rather, the intent is to guide you through the process of developing your own administrative model for an instructional coaching initiative that maximizes both individual and collective teacher capacity. Leading experts in the field of coaching provide a wealth of outstanding literature that clearly defines and describes coaching. You can learn **why** schools and districts include coaching as an integral component of their professional development programs by studying the work of Knight (2007, 2009, 2011), Killion and Harrison (2006), and Barkley (2010). Each of these authors combines research on the effectiveness of instructional coaching as a professional learning model with their extensive field experience as professional developers and "coaches of coaches." Costa and Garmston (2002) discuss the rationale for cognitive coaching, whose initial purpose is "to enhance an individual's capacity for self-directed learning through self-management, self-monitoring, and self-modification" (p. 5), in relation to the principles of constructivism, the "theory of learning based on a belief that human beings have an innate quest to make meaning from their experiences" (p. 389).

To help you understand what coaches do, Killion and Harrison (2006) identify and explain the 10 roles of coaches that include "a) resource provider, b) data coach, c) curriculum specialist, d) instructional specialist, e) classroom supporter, f) mentor, g) learning facilitator,

h) school leader, i) catalyst for change, and j) learner" (p. 28). Knight (2007) describes what coaching looks like and explores various coaching roles and responsibilities. In *Unmistakable Impact* (2011), Knight features a chapter describing "how instructional coaches (ICs) can support and stimulate the learning that is at the heart of Impact Schools" (p. 91). Barkley (2010) defines instructional coaching, the role of an instructional coach, and the skills required for coaching. He stresses the importance of creating a pervasive coaching culture within the learning organization to support and strengthen quality teaching.

There are also a number of great resources on specific **coaching models** used in schools today. Allen and LeBlanc (2005) describe their 2+2 *Performance Appraisal Model* of peer coaching this way: "2+2 for teachers is a concept of classroom observation that focuses on the power of feedback, encouragement, discussion and discourse, and the importance of perspective and collaboration in the improvement of instruction" (p. 105), offering a remedy to the issues of isolation, stagnation, discouragement, and uncertainty among teachers. B. Tschannen-Moran and Tschannen-Moran (2010) incorporate the use of story, empathy, inquiry, and design in their *evocative coaching* model. By developing strong relationships based on honesty and trust, evocative coaches help teachers discover the motivation and power to improve their own professional classroom performance. Content-focused coaching models are described in the works of Morse (2009), Sadder and Nidus (2009), and Moxley (2006). In the book *Coaching Approaches & Perspectives* (2009), Knight synthesizes descriptions of a variety of coaching models by including contributions from experts in the areas of literacy coaching, data coaching, cognitive coaching, differentiated coaching, and leadership coaching.

Bon Voyage

Do you remember Bob Dylan's 1962 song "Blowin' in the Wind"? This song has meant many things to many people in the 50-plus years it has been around, but it serves to illustrate an important point if you visualize the road, the man walking down it, the wind blowing . . . an isolated and melancholy picture. Then visualize another person coming out to join him, cheering him on, helping him navigate the rough and smooth terrain as an equal partner. That is coaching. We walk the most important road in the world—the road that is the future of our children. Let's make the journey together as learning partners.

Building an Instructional Coaching Program for Maximum Capacity
1. Research coaching and coaching models. Reach out to others (coaches, coaching champions) in the professional community. (Chapter 1)
2. Select a "champion team" who will develop the coaching initiative and will support coaching. (Chapter 2)
3. Develop a shared vision of instructional coaching for your school or district. (Chapter 2)
4. Align your vision of instructional coaching with your school or district's vision. (Chapter 2)
5. Develop an administrative model for coaching. (Chapter 2)
6. Develop your assessment plan for the coaching initiative. Know what you will evaluate and how you will do it. (Chapter 3)
7. Know the five characteristics of great coaches prior to hiring and assigning, and use them to develop a recruitment strategy. Interview and hire coaches. (Chapter 4)
8. Determine preservice training needs for administrators and supervisors and develop a learning plan. (Chapter 5)
9. Determine preservice training needs for newly hired instructional coaches and develop a learning plan for the first of the school year as part of a long-term comprehensive model of ongoing professional learning and support. (Chapter 6)
10. Plan for opportunities for regular collaboration among and between coaches and teachers after coaches begin. (Chapter 7)
11. Develop a model of ongoing learning and support for instructional coaches. (Chapter 8)
12. Evaluate your coaching program and make necessary adjustments to sustain, change, abandon, or reimagine your coaching initiative. (Chapters 3 and 9)

2

Dead Reckoning

Beginning With the End in Mind

"In the midst of this chopping sea of civilized life, such are the clouds and storms and quicksands and thousand-and-one items to be allowed for, that a man has to live, if he would not founder and go to the bottom and not make his port at all, by dead reckoning, and he must be a great calculator indeed who succeeds. Simplify, simplify."

—Thoreau (2011)

How many times those "thousand-and-one items" in schools or in life take the place of the main thing! As Thoreau reminds us, the only way to keep from drowning in the details is to know your destination. On any journey, we must simplify our actions by doing what is important. *Dead reckoning*, a navigational term that refers to estimating present location by projecting the course and speed from a known past location, can also be used to estimate where you will be in the future. Your vision for the future may be a distant shore, but simplifying an organization's actions by dead reckoning puts everyone on course and allows you to make key decisions as you move forward.

The concept of dead reckoning is important in designing and developing any instructional improvement initiative—we must assess where we have been and where we are now and compare it to where we want to be. This is the only way we will be able to assess how successful our voyage has been. Guskey (2000) points out the steps you must take at this point to make sure you will be able to assess the effectiveness of any professional learning endeavor. First, you must create a purpose statement or vision that is clear. Second, you will make sure this vision is worthwhile—that it supports the vision of your organization. This chapter will help you do both of these things. Finally, you will have to develop a plan to evaluate whether your goals have been met. Chapter 3 will help you do this. Just as a teacher must make sure his or her lesson objectives are "measurable," you must keep this in mind as you articulate your goals.

> "Probably the two greatest failures of leaders are indecisiveness in times of urgent need for action and dead certainty that they are right in times of complexity."
>
> —Michael Fullan (2008)

Let Go of Certainty

Dead reckoning is not dead certainty. Coaching and teaching are people-work, and people are messy. When my first child was a baby, a friend gave me a book with this quote by John Wilmot: "Before I married, I had three theories about raising children and no children. Now, I have three children and no theories." This could just as easily be said of coaching. Just as every child is different, every teacher, principal, and coach is different, and therefore every coaching program is different. There are many books on approaches to coaching, but we have personally never seen two coaching initiatives that are exactly alike. Parents may read sound research on child rearing, and they may listen to the sage advice of other parents, but the one thing that carries you through raising kids is the core vision for your family that helps guide you when you make decisions. Coaching cannot be implemented as if you were following a recipe any more than a script can take the place of a good lesson plan. You must know where you are and where you are going, but you must accept that your journey is uniquely your own. Be wary of any "program" that stipulates every step your coaches should take. While this may be comforting, it is not sustainable.

Clarify Your Vision

Covey (1989) cautions that "the extent to which you begin with the end in mind often determines whether or not you are able to create a successful enterprise" (p. 99). The "end" is the vision of where you want to be in the future; your mission is getting there. Schools and districts are in a continuous school-improvement cycle in which creating and communicating a vision statement is crucial. A vision statement, simply put, is a picture of what an organization hopes to become—its highest destiny. Your mission is the "overall direction that emerges from the vision, a specific agenda, or to-do list that guides the development of goals that will in turn dictate the day-to-day behavior of the organization" (McEwan-Adkins, 2009, p. 58). Your goals, then, are the specific steps you will take to carry out your mission.

Your school or district vision should revolve around teaching and learning, and be supported by a professional learning vision. A coaching program is one facet of your professional learning, and it exists, like everything else in an organization should, to get you closer to your vision. Your first step in visioning for your program is to look at the overall vision of your district or school system. Within that vision should be the vision or visions of individual schools, and just as the individual schools determine their vision in relation to the overall vision of the district, you will need to determine how your coaching program will support professional learning and align with the larger vision.

As you can see, your vision of coaching will be difficult to establish if you do not have a clear school and/or district vision. If your district sees itself as one in which all students graduate ready for postsecondary education and your school sees itself as a place where all students are active and engaged learners to prepare for postsecondary education, then the vision for your coaching program is one

Figure 2.1   Coaching Vision and Goals

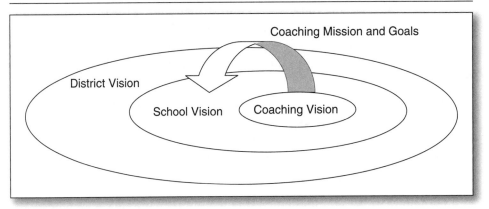

in which coaches support all teachers in actively engaging learners in their classrooms every day. This vision, then, will drive every other decision you make about the coaching program. Your coaching program's mission should be to carry out at least part of the mission of your school or district.

> *"A mission cannot be impersonal; it has to have deep meaning, be something you believe in—something you know is right. A fundamental responsibility of leadership is to make sure that everybody knows the mission, understands it, lives it."*
>
> —Peter Drucker et al. (2008)

Your vision and mission are only meaningful if they are meaningful to the people in your organization. Drucker and colleagues (2008) write that once we have determined our vision and mission, we must identify our customers—those stakeholders who value the work and the results of our organization. Instructional coaching has stakeholders at all levels of the organization. As with any educational aim, the fundamental, desired result with instructional coaching is increased *student* achievement. However, instructional coaches work primarily with *teachers* and *administrators* to assist them as they work directly with students. As you consider the vision for your instructional coaching program, you must determine how your instructional coaching program can best serve your teachers and administrators as they do the primary work of the school—teaching students.

When considering implementing an instructional coaching program, listen to the customers in your organization who work with or are affected by the professional learning approaches you use.

Stakeholders at the district level may include the director of professional learning, instructional coordinators and supervisors, instructional technology specialists, and representative principals and teachers. At the school level, they might include the principal, assistant principals, and teacher leaders. The district professional learning coordinator and instructional supervisors can also provide valuable support and insight to creating your vision and measuring the effectiveness of your school's professional learning model.

Figure Your Present Location

If you are going to advance from a known past location, you have to set a "fix" or a reading of where you are now. Essentially, you want to assess the impact of your organization's professional learning model on teacher collaboration, teacher efficacy, and teacher effect. How well does your current professional learning model increase your teachers' capacity and resourcefulness for working together to increase student achievement? The assessment of your current professional learning model can be expanded to capture additional qualitative data and to include quantitative data. Surveys, needs assessments, rating scales, interviews, and focus groups provide a wealth of perceptual information.

According to Drucker and colleagues (2008), "self-assessment is a commitment to developing yourself and your organization as a leader. You will expand your vision by listening to your customers . . . " (p. 5). When considering professional learning initiatives, the teachers and their supervisors are your customers, because they are the individuals who benefit from the learning in terms of more successful teaching experiences. Survey teachers, administrators, and other stakeholders regarding their satisfaction with the professional learning in your organization. Determine their prior knowledge about coaching and their interest in coaching as a component of your professional learning model. This will help you see areas of professional learning that need to be strengthened and give you a good idea of how much additional knowledge about coaching teachers might need before they participate in it.

It is important as you listen to these voices that you judge your current programs compared to Learning Forward's (2011) *Standards for Professional Learning*. Look at the professional learning model used in your school or district in terms of context (where the learning occurs), process (how the learning occurs), and content (the learning itself). Review the definition of professional learning from Learning Forward (2011): *"a comprehensive, sustained, intensive and collaborative approach to improving teachers' and principals' effectiveness in raising student achievement"* (para. 2, emphasis added). Then, answer the following questions:

1. Does our current professional learning model encourage and foster the use of professional learning communities?

2. Does our current professional learning model support adult learning and collaboration by providing our teachers and administrators the knowledge and skills needed to collaborate?

3. Is our current professional learning model designed to incorporate a variety of adult learning strategies?

4. Does our current professional learning model include *job-embedded* learning opportunities?

5. Most importantly, does our current professional learning model support and align with our student achievement goals?

If you can answer *yes* to each of these questions, you should be able to produce evidence of the effectiveness of each component of your professional learning model. If you answer *no* to some or all of them, you have steps to take to make your professional learning more effective.

> *"To abandon anything is always bitterly resisted. People in any organization are always attached to the obsolete—the things that should have worked but did not, the things that once were productive and no longer are."*
>
> —Peter Drucker et al. (2008)

Strengthen or Abandon

Before you embark on your coaching journey, it is critical to look closely at your *current* teacher professional learning programs. Does your current professional learning model support your school's or district's mission? Or is it just a "thousand-and-one items that must be allowed for" complete with endless "shotgun approach" workshops that touch on a myriad of strategies and concepts but have little impact on teacher practice? All aspects of your professional learning model should be designed to support the vision, mission, and goals of your organization. When you find the actions that are supporting the mission and vision, strengthen them. Coaching can be one way to do that. Workshops that are valuable become even more valuable when followed up with coached implementation in the classroom.

It is just as important to *stop* doing those things that do not support your vision as it is to *start* new programs and initiatives or *streng*then initiatives that do support it. You must ask yourself if you need to abandon "the things that have outlived their usefulness and their capacity to contribute" (Drucker et al., 2008, p. 68). Are there facets of your professional learning model that no longer contribute (or perhaps never have) to teacher collaboration, teacher efficacy, and teacher effect? Is your organization holding on to an ineffective model of professional learning for tradition's sake? Letting go of things, even things that are not working, can be a daunting challenge. "For an organization to maintain a focus on its highest priorities, it must simplify and repeatedly clarify them so that everyone in the organization knows implicitly what to do and *what not to do*" (Schmoker, 2011, p. 16). All professional learning is expensive. Coaching, because it is human resource intensive, is no different. Can you reallocate other professional learning funds to pay for coaching salaries? Are there some things you are doing that are no longer effective that can be abandoned and the savings used for coaching?

REFLECT: As you envision implementing a coaching initiative in your school or district, what are some professional learning approaches you can abandon? What prevents you from doing so?

Determine How Far You Have to Go

According to a report released by the national accreditation agency AdvancEd (2010), spending a lot of time on the details of "word-smithing" a vision and mission statement is less important than "connecting the vision to the core function of schools and school systems—teaching and learning" (p. 7). In other words, the vision is your destination, but if you are going to navigate by dead reckoning, you have to connect where you are currently in the areas of teaching and learning with where you want to be and determine how far you have to go to get there. Then you need to ask yourself if coaching will help you get where you need to be. As a form of professional learning, coaching should align with your school's or district's professional learning goals. To do this, evaluate your current professional learning plan, your professional learning budget, your use of PLCs, and school-based and job-embedded professional learning opportunities already in place in your school or district. Will coaching complement what you are doing? Is it too soon to try to begin? Should some groundwork take place in the form of other collaborative learning activities?

Ask yourself and your colleagues, "Will implementing a coaching model support our school's or district's vision? And if so, do we have the basic resources to pursue it?" If the answer to these questions is *yes*, then you are ready to take the next steps in developing a coaching initiative for your school or district.

Move From Vision to Plan

One drawback of dead reckoning is that it does not take winds and currents into effect. It is navigation based solely on where you are and where you want to be, so any assessment errors made along the way can be cumulative. The same is true with visioning . . . to make your vision a reality and to live out your mission, you must have a plan. A plan consists of goals, objectives, action steps, resources, and a continual cycle of assessment and refinement.

Plan From the Top Down or Bottom Up?

A coaching program can be initiated at several levels: district, school, or even a department or grade group within a school. In many cases, the coaching program is a top-down decision—the district leadership decides coaching should be the direction for professional learning in the district, and they make a plan to implement it. Other coaching programs are planned at the school level, when a principal decides to provide school-based professional learning in this manner. Sometimes, coaching is truly bottom up: A group of teachers decides to experiment with coaching within their team and act as coaches for each other. They might have a reading specialist or Title I teacher who wants to transform her role into that of a coach. This "bottom-up" planning can be effective, but only with the principal's leadership and support. The principal must be the instructional leader in the school, and whether the initiative originates with the district or with the desire of a group of teachers, the principal is the key to effective planning and implementation. According to Knight (2011), "when a principal is the instructional leader in absentia, teaching practices may be unsystematically implemented by some and not at all by others, and school improvement may progress in an incoherent manner that is troubling and confusing for teachers and students" (p. 97). Whether you are a teacher, team leader, or district supervisor who wants to start a coaching program, you must enroll the principal as a partner early in the initiative.

Start With a Champion Team

Ideally, a coaching initiative will come from a school- or district-level team—a professional learning community, an intensive learning team, a school or district improvement team—that is passionate about improving professional learning, collaboration, and student achievement. If this team is not already in place, you should form a group of coaching champions that we like to call a "champion team." The team will begin the planning process for coaching by identifying some long-term goals and working backward to identify action steps along the way. A champion team should include various committed stakeholders and may include teachers, principals, instructional supervisors, professional developers, and individuals with backgrounds in special education, English Language Learners, and various content areas and grade groups that will be impacted by the coaching initiative.

When the team is in place, you must determine your collective knowledge of coaching and formulate a shared vision of coaching in your school or district. You will clarify goals for coaching, focus and refocus, and never be satisfied! Make sure everyone develops the same picture of coaching and that there is a collective mind regarding the purpose of your initiative.

> **REFLECT:** Consider the human resources at your disposal. Brainstorm some names of individuals who may serve on your champion team.

Divide the Labor

Setting up a coaching initiative is a lot of work. The champion team must divide the tasks involved. These tasks include but are not limited to: developing, administering, and analyzing stakeholder surveys; researching and reporting on the coaching literature; networking with other schools and districts to learn from other programs;

determining initial and ongoing professional learning needs; determining how to evaluate coaches and the coaching program; developing job descriptions; advertising for coaches; and serving on coach selection committees. This, of course, is just the beginning. The champion team should be involved every step of the way in training coaches and administrators, collecting data, and troubleshooting as your program gets underway.

Do Your Research

The coaching plan will require visioning and research specific to coaching. Although coaching has been around for decades, the published research on coaching has grown exponentially only in the last few years. Deploy members of your champion team to investigate the published information about coaching as well as firsthand accounts from practitioners. In the Chapter 2 resource section, you will find a chart that is useful for sharing of research information with your colleagues. One of our most valuable research experiences was spending several days in professional learning with coaching teams from Salem-Kiser school district in Oregon. From them, we got a firsthand account of what coaching was and some advantages and potential pitfalls that might occur. If there are other coaching programs nearby, we recommend a visit and an observation. One of the delights of coaching is the widespread willingness of coaches and others who work with coaching to share their knowledge—it is part of the coaching model, after all—and you will be able to learn from their experiences! Remember, however, that no two schools or districts are alike. We all come to this experience with different histories, skills, and resources.

Determine Where Coaching Will Fit in With Your Current Initiatives

Your champion team can take a closer look at the vision of your district, the needs of your professional learning program, and the financial resources of your school or district and determine whether a coaching initiative is a viable way to reach your goals. The beauty of coaching is that it is so flexible. It can be developed in a myriad of ways to support the vision of your school or district. Just like no two classrooms are identical, no two coaching programs need to look exactly alike! At this point, it may be a good idea to create and post a copy of your district vision and mission near your workspace or desk. You will be referring to it quite frequently!

Develop an Administrative Model

At this stage of the process, you have some decisions to make that will influence how your coaching program will be organized. The champion team should review their research, needs assessments, vision, and mission and answer the following questions:

1. What are the specific goals of your coaching program?

There are many outcomes for coaching, but primarily, the goals of a coaching program are increased student achievement and improved professional collaboration (Killion & Harrison, 2006). A principal or district may have more specific goals, including implementation of a specific district or school initiative. Clarifying what you wish to achieve will help you make decisions about the type of coaching you wish to implement. It may also be helpful to establish short- and long-range benchmarks for assessing progress toward your goals. See Chapter 2 resources for an example.

2. What is the role of a coach in your coaching program?

The literature describes many different types of coaching, including cognitive coaching, content coaching, data coaching, literacy coaching, and instructional coaching, among others. All of these approaches have been successful in various locations and situations. It is important to choose a coaching model or a blend of several coaching models that best meet your particular needs.

3. Will the coaches work for one school or the district? If the district, how many schools will they serve?

The answer to this question is at the heart of your administrative model. If a district wants instructional coaching to implement a districtwide initiative, it may choose to hire and deploy coaches from the district office who work in two or more schools. Sometimes this approach is chosen simply because the funds are inadequate to support hiring a coach for each school. School-based coaches (1:1 model) are the norm in some districts, and coaches in this situation have the advantage of building close relationships with the staff of their assigned schools. According to Killion and Harrison (2006), "Principals typically prefer having coaches assigned full-time to their school so that the coach develops a deep understanding of the school's culture and provides sustained support over time" (p. 101). However, both approaches have advantages. District-based coaches who are assigned to two schools may forge collaborative bonds between teachers in different locations who are facing similar challenges. They may be able to facilitate horizontal and vertical planning in "feeder-school" situations. District-based coaches may have a greater exposure to the initiatives and goals of the district and may provide consistent coaching across a district. School-based coaches in 1:1 models have more time to work with individual teachers and to develop a wider and deeper knowledge of school initiatives and needs. You may wish to create your own hybrid approach by hiring pools of district coaches who are then selected by principals to be a "best fit" in their schools. Two principals may decide to team together to share a coach and may even coach each other for their own professional learning.

4. Who will supervise the coaches and who will participate in hiring?

In general, 1:1 school-based coaches are supervised by their principals and district-based coaches are supervised by district personnel. At the district level, this can be an instructional supervisor, a professional learning director, or another staff member. Ideally, this will be a person who has good rapport with the principals with whom the coaches will work.

The decision regarding who participates in hiring instructional coaches is dependent to some degree upon the administrative model that is chosen. District coaches are selected by the district and school-based coaches at the school level. In either case, it is best if a person from each level of the organization participates in the hiring decision. For example, if the administrative model is a school-based, 1:1 model, the principal may invite teachers and district personnel to participate in the hiring decision. If it is district based, representative teachers and principals should have input. It is always important to review the contracts, labor agreements, and hiring policies and procedures of your district before making a decision on how to select a coach.

5. How will coaches be matched with schools?

If a coach is selected at the school level, then the specific needs and culture of the school are taken into account when hiring. The principal in this case must decide whether to hire from within or from outside the school faculty, and there are pros and cons to this that are discussed in greater length in Chapter 4.

If the coach will be hired at the district level, an important decision will be where each coach will be placed. If resources are limited and a coach cannot be hired for each school, a viable alternative might be to place coaches in the schools with the greatest need. Many districts provide coaches for Title I schools (schools with high poverty), schools that are experiencing failing test scores, or schools in which there have been administrative or personnel changes. The commitment of the principal to coaching should also be considered here. If a principal is unwilling to support coaching, we have found that it is almost impossible for a coach to be effective. Limited coaching resources should be allocated to the places where leadership truly desires a collaborative culture among teachers.

When a district determines which schools will get coaches, then they must decide what qualities are necessary for the coach in each particular school. It is very important that school-based personnel are involved in this decision. They can brainstorm a list of experiences or areas of expertise that would provide a good fit with their school. In describing organizations that move from *Good to Great* (2001), Collins emphasizes the importance of getting the right people on the bus, but also getting the right person on the right *seat* in the bus. Coaches that might be particularly effective in one school may be less so in another. That is why it is crucial to a coach's success that she is placed where she can be most effective. Key to this decision is the personality fit between principal and coach. It is important that the coach and principal have compatible or complementary work and communication styles.

6. Who will champion the coaches?

Regardless of who will supervise the coaches, if more than one school in a district is implementing coaching, we believe a district-level person or team must be in place to champion the coaches. Killion and Harrison (2006) define the coaching champion as "someone who will provide day-to-day guidance for coaches, intervene during breakdowns of policy and practice, and facilitate sensitive interactions between coaches and principals" (p. 111). Furthermore, the coach champion is "the guardian of the coaching program to ensure that teachers and students receive the maximum benefit from coaches' work" (p. 112). The coaching champions may be supervisors as well, but this is not necessary. They may be district staff who serve as liaisons between the district office and the school-based coach, or they may be the district-level supervisors of the coaches if the coaches are assigned to several schools. Key to their role is facilitating communication between the coaches and appropriate district personnel and between coaches and principals when communication breaks down. They will also facilitate initial and ongoing professional learning for the coaches. It is our experience that two or more coaching champions are ideal. They must model the model by participating in coach professional learning and by coaching each other and the coaches!

7. What rules and regulations will affect the hiring, placement, evaluation, and tenure of coaches?

Chapter 3 identifies specific criteria for evaluating coaches, but at this early stage in your planning process, you should consider what local restrictions exist that govern how coaches can be hired, evaluated, and terminated. By contract or labor agreement, will coaches be considered teachers, or are they in some other category of employee? Are specific licensure requirements in place for coaches in your state? If so, do they identify a specific evaluation model or hiring protocol? Do transfer rules apply to coaching positions? Can a teacher be temporarily assigned to a coaching position and have rights to return to his or her prior job? Can coaches attain tenure in their positions? These are questions that applicants might ask and conditions you should be familiar with as you design your program.

8. How will district–coach and principal–coach communication occur?

Good communication, whether in a school or in a family, does not happen by accident. You must create a thoughtful communication plan between your coaches and principals, the district and the principal, and the district and the coaching champion. Ideally, a coach will communicate daily with her principal, but this may not always be possible. A set meeting time and place should be instituted so that all parties have time to listen to each other. Likewise, coaches should meet regularly with their champions.

The basis of good communication is trust. For this reason, a detailed confidentiality plan should be agreed upon and communicated to all stakeholders. What may a coach tell a principal or district official about a teacher? In some districts, contracts stipulate that data from coaching interactions cannot be used in the evaluation process. Whether or not this is the case, the integrity of the coaching program depends upon a trusting relationship between teacher and coach. Coaches, principals, and district leaders must establish what information will be shared and then communicate this agreement to the teachers.

9. With whom will the coaches work within the school?

In small schools with a 1:1 coaching model, a coach may be able to work with all the teachers. In larger schools, especially at the secondary level, coaches may be assigned to specific departments based on subject area expertise, or they may work with teams of teachers instead of individuals. This decision will greatly influence the kind of person you will select as a coach—do you want a generalist who can apply her excellent skills to any subject or grade level, or will you look for a person who has specific content area expertise? Do you want someone who is especially good in one-on-one interactions or someone who has more specific skills in managing groups and teams? Ideally, you will have a coach with both, but if not, this must be taken into consideration. Do you want your coaches to work primarily with new teachers or experienced teachers? Do you wish to build capacity with your top teachers first, or do you want to use coaches to assist with teachers who have been unsuccessful in the past? Based on our vision for our coaching program, our preference is to begin with the best teachers—those who have the most invested in their profession and who are most likely to benefit from coaching. We found that this was the best use of resources in our situation. In many cases, however, principals asked coaches to work with struggling teachers, and great outcomes were achieved.

10. How long will the coaches serve in their positions?

Some professional coaches serve in that capacity for most of their careers. Others serve only a few years and then return to the classroom. There are advantages to both models. Coaches who return to the classroom every few years avoid losing touch with the daily challenges of classroom teaching and often have more credibility with teachers. However, coaching is a skill like any other that is honed with time and practice. A good, well-trained, and experienced coach can be extremely valuable to your school. It can take 3 years for a coach to hit her stride with a faculty, so we recommend that coaches stay in their positions for at least that long.

11. What are the district policies and parameters for coaches?

Before your coaching program is in place, it is important that all stakeholders, including the coaches themselves, understand their role in the school. It is not uncommon to talk to coaches who feel they spend most of their time doing clerical, administrative, or tutoring work. Of course, in a school, a time will come when everyone must assume different tasks to get a job done, but this should be the exception, not the rule. Substituting, tutoring, cafeteria monitoring, and bus duty must not interfere with the coach's primary responsibilities. This must be communicated to principals, teachers, staff, and parents.

Anticipate the Squall

A squall is a sudden, violent wind that tends to pop up where you least expect it. Good leaders expect the unexpected and anticipate potential areas where problems may crop up. Your champion team, especially if it is composed of a variety of stakeholders of varying backgrounds, can brainstorm a pretty comprehensive list of potential problems with coaching. You may not be able to identify every potentiality, but you will have many of them, and you can design your program to avoid some of them and have contingency plans to deal with others. Some squalls that might come out in a brainstorming session might include

- How do we respond to resistance to coaching from other leaders?
- What happens if there is a severe breach of trust in a coaching relationship?
- What happens if a principal intentionally sabotages a coaching program?
- What if a coach is not accepted at a school and, after a period of time, is having no progress?
- What if a principal is using a coach as a tutor or substitute instead of as a coach?
- What if everyone loves the coach, but no improvement is seen in instruction or teacher collaboration over time?

Summary

To avoid complexity and keep things simple, a good coaching implementation plan based on evidence is important. Steps in developing your plan include the following:

1. Letting go of certainty

2. Clarifying your vision and mission

3. Figuring out your current status

4. Deciding what to strengthen or abandon

5. Determining how far you have to go to reach your vision

6. Moving from your vision to a plan

7. Developing a champion team that can divide labor and research the topic

8. Developing an administrative model for your program

9. Anticipating the "squalls" or difficulties that might arise

When the squalls come, sometimes all we need to do to find our way is to simplify. We cannot get too busy with the details to see the big picture. When things get confusing, we always go back to our vision . . . the vision of our system, school, and coaching program. Our plan is important, but we have to accept that our plan is a plan and not a law book. . . . It should be used to guide us and simplify our work, but we must be ready to adjust it when its usefulness is outlived.

REFLECT: Read the following quote from Fullan:

Leadership must create conditions that value learning as both individual and collective good. Leaders must create environments in which individuals expect to have their personal ideas and practices subjected to the scrutiny of their colleagues, and in which groups expect to have their shared conceptions of practice subjected to the scrutiny of individuals. (Fullan, 2001, p. 130)

What constitutes "conditions that value learning as both individual and collective good?" What are some practical ways an administrator or teacher leader create these conditions?

Building an Instructional Coaching Program for Maximum Capacity

1. Research coaching and coaching models. Reach out to others (coaches, coaching champions) in the professional community. (Chapter 1)

2. Select a "champion team" who will develop the coaching initiative and will support coaching. (Chapter 2

3. Develop a shared vision of instructional coaching for your school or district. (Chapter 2)

4. Align your vision of instructional coaching with your school or district's vision. (Chapter 2)

5. Develop an administrative model for coaching. (Chapter 2)

6. **Develop your assessment plan for the coaching initiative. Know what you will evaluate and how you will do it. (Chapter 3)**

7. Know the five characteristics of great coaches prior to hiring and assigning, and use them to develop a recruitment strategy. Interview and hire coaches. (Chapter 4)

8. Determine preservice training needs for administrators and supervisors and develop a learning plan. (Chapter 5)

9. Determine preservice training needs for newly hired instructional coaches and develop a learning plan for the first of the school year as part of a long-term comprehensive model of ongoing professional learning and support. (Chapter 6)

10. Plan for opportunities for regular collaboration among and between coaches and teachers after coaches begin. (Chapter 7)

11. Develop a model of ongoing learning and support for instructional coaches. (Chapter 8)

12. **Evaluate your coaching program and make necessary adjustments to sustain, change, abandon, or reimagine your coaching initiative. (Chapters 3 and 9)**

3

Sounding the Depths

Using Data for Reflecting, Refining, and Celebrating

Over the years, educators have encountered the occasional "ship-wreck" as programs and policies are adopted, inadequately implemented, and subsequently left to sink. Without an evaluation plan, we lack adequate information to gauge effectiveness, to promote meaningful reflection on practice, and to communicate success.

Before we can prepare the ship for sailing, we must make sure we have all the navigational tools we need to know where we are, calculate where we are going, and celebrate how far we have come.

> *"Without feedback, we shrivel into routines and develop hard shells that keep newness out. We don't survive for long."*
>
> —Margaret Wheatley and
> Myron Kellner-Rogers (1999b)

On any journey, you want to know how far you have come and how far you have to go. When my children were little and we would go on a long road-trip vacation, they would love to annoy me by asking in singsong unison from the backseat, "Are we there yet?" After a few hundred miles, they would finally settle down and the drive would become peaceful. The moment I sighed with relief, one of them would shout out, "How much longer?" And the questions would begin again. Sometimes, in exasperation, their dad and I would tell them (after a 4- or 5-hour drive) that we had left something at home and had to turn around and go back!! Very young, they developed a keen sense of irony but a poor sense of distance.

When you implement change in your organization, you may feel you are being bombarded with a chorus of "Are we there yet?" Your staff and you want to know if you are going in the right direction and how close you are getting to your goals. School board members, parents, the community, and students all want to know that the changes that have been implemented, sometimes at great cost, are leading toward student achievement. And everyone wants to know whether you've forgotten something important and will have to turn back!

Identify Program Goals and Coaching Goals

In Chapter 2, you considered your vision and set specific program goals. Everyone's goals are somewhat different, but the expectations of any typical coaching program are twofold: You expect to see increased **academic performance** and improved **professional collaboration** (Killion & Harrison, 2006). In addition to these goals, your school or district may also have more detailed expectations. It is important to look closely at your program goals and to ask yourself what kinds of information you will need to assess whether you have met or exceeded your goals.

When we began our coaching program, our goal was to increase student preparedness for postsecondary education and to develop a culture of coaching that maximized the capacity of the teachers in our district. We wanted to see more and deeper development of professional learning communities (PLCs) and peer coaching. We had gone through a backward planning process, starting with student achievement, and we believed that reflective and collaborative practice on the part of our teachers and administrators would lead to teaching that was centered on individual student success. We wanted our teachers to experience what Barkley (2010) identified as three outcomes of coaching: celebration, options, and conscious practice. We wanted to develop a way to assess our progress toward our vision. Also, we knew we would have to have very specific goals for our coaches and an explicit way of determining their progress toward those goals.

Determine Your Purpose

It is very helpful for the coach and for those who evaluate the coach and program to take a fresh look at evidence of progress on a regular and predetermined basis. Perhaps the most important use of coaching data is to have some concrete starting point to begin a discussion about what is working and what needs to be addressed in your organization. Stakeholder perceptual data are especially important. Just as a teacher must do in a classroom, we must constantly check the validity of our assumptions—are we connecting the right dots? Is the strategy working?

It may sound simple, but it is important to consider and perhaps rank the different kinds of evaluation you will want your data to enable. Different organizational and sometimes political considerations may come into play in this determination. You must have the purpose of your assessment plan firmly in mind, or you will end up with a lot of information that is time-consuming to manage and impossible to evaluate. Some purposes for data gathering and assessment are the following.

To Evaluate the Program

You collect formative data that will let you know if the program is meeting its goals. These are the kind of data that you will want to review and share regularly with administrators and coaches in order to make necessary adjustments, as well as to demonstrate program value to board members, administrators, teachers, and the coaches themselves. Districts or schools need to show documentation that the plan and policies regarding the program are followed. Coaching programs that have used federal, state, or other grant funds to develop or expand coaching programs will require detailed data to demonstrate compliance.

To Evaluate Principals or Other Leaders of the Coaching Program

An often-overlooked area of data collection revolves around the amount of support provided by school-level or district-level personnel. Principals should have a record of activities they conduct in support of the coach and the program in general, and coaches and teachers should be able to indicate their perception of the level of support coaching receives. These activities should be a part of the administrator's evaluation process.

To Evaluate the Coach

You must also collect formative data to provide feedback to the coach concerning her individual performance. The pedagogical skills, content area knowledge, and coaching skills of your coaches have a huge effect on your program, and how coaches demonstrate those skills is paramount. Your job description and performance standards should outline what you expect from your coaches. In turn, you need to identify how you will evaluate meeting those standards.

Certain types of coach data collection are done to fulfill organization obligations. This might include logs, schedules, meeting agendas, and leave forms. These types of data are needed for accountability purposes and are sometimes also helpful in diagnosing problems in the program. For example, one coach we worked with seemed to be making limited progress at one of her schools. A review of the school calendar and the snow days that occurred revealed that she had less than half the number of coaching days as she had had in her other school. Part of the problem was being assigned to that school on Mondays and Fridays: Two Mondays during the winter were holidays, and Fridays tended to be days when schoolwide events that disrupted teaching schedules took place. We made some schedule adjustments and the problem began to correct itself.

In most cases, some sort of formal evaluation process must be done in order to fulfill teacher contractual obligations. Some school districts have very specific requirements for teacher evaluations, and in those cases, you must be careful to follow the law, contract, or policy explicitly. In the absence of a mandated evaluation plan specific to coaches, it may be helpful to create an evaluation tool that gives the coach more specific feedback about his or her performance regarding coaching. Killion and Harrison (2006) recommend that districts include observations of coaches engaged in their work as a part of the evaluation process.

> In this book, our concern with the evaluation of coaching is from a program-improvement perspective. You are evaluating coaching performance with the goal of using the data to continually improve it and to celebrate its successes. We do not intend to tackle the (rare) problem of personnel issues leading to the reprimand of an employee.

To Monitor the Effectiveness of Individual Teacher–Coach Relationships

The coach must collect formative data concerning her individual coaching interactions with a teacher so that together they can make a decision to continue or modify their interactions. In reviewing coaching schedules with a new coach, I noticed that she was working with one particular teacher almost exclusively. Because of the detailed information the coach had recorded concerning the number, topic, and type of coaching interactions, she was able to reflect on the progress they were making and realized that she should have a similar reflective conversation with the teacher. Out of their conversation, they decided to bring peer coaching into their work, reduce their one-on-one work, and involve a greater number of teachers who could benefit from the experience.

REFLECT   Use the following questions to help you determine your purpose for data collection.

- What purposes are most important for your data collection and assessment plan?
- Which do you think will be the most difficult to achieve?
- How frequently will you need feedback in order to evaluate the program, the leaders, and the coaches?

Determine the Measures to Meet Your Purposes and Goals

Designing the assessment plan is very much like designing a lesson plan. The teacher wants to measure the growth of the individual student *and* she wants feedback on the entire class in order to modify and adapt instruction. The teacher determines what success will look like before the lesson is taught. She designs formative and summative assessments to provide information about how close the students are to success. The teacher gives feedback to students and parents and makes changes in practice based on the data. Additionally, the teacher knows she is accountable and must have documentation that she is fulfilling her legal, policy, and ethical obligations to her students, school, school system, state accreditation agencies, and, in many cases, the federal government. Just as in a lesson plan, the designers of a coaching program have some very specific purposes for collecting data about the program and about the individual coaches.

When designing our assessment plan, we scoured published resources to find instruments to help us collect and manage data about individual coaching interactions and coach time usage. In addition to fulfilling the roles of instructional coaches, we also were concerned that coaches spend time on several district initiatives that were already in place, such as brain-based instructional methods and character education. To monitor work on these initiatives, we asked coaches to keep records of the *number* and *kinds* of coaching interactions they engaged in, as well as logs of their time usage and counts of the numbers of teachers they coached. See Chapter 3 resources for a sample coaching interactions form.

> *"In shallow water, both the coach and the teacher feel safe. They can touch bottom. They have a limited perspective of what it means to swim because they can still stand. In deep water, however, both the coach and the teacher, unless they are competent swimmers, are outside their comfort zone."*
>
> —Joellen Killion (2009, pp. 25–26)

In our second year, we refocused our goals and reevaluated the sorts of data we were collecting. There was some indication from the data that our coaches were spending more time on *coaching shallow* activities, such as resource providing and presenting professional learning sessions, than *coaching deep* activities such as lesson study and coplanning. We also noticed that some coaches were interacting with most if not all teachers in a building. Others were coaching deeply with just a few. Looking at coaching interaction logs reminded us of a song we sang as children called "Deep and Wide" that had hand motions showing depth and width and a "fountain flowing, deep and wide." It occurred to us that our coaches needed to engage in deep *and* wide coaching. If we wanted a culture of coaching, deep instructional coaching had to occur widely with *many* teachers in a building—a veritable tidal wave of coaching culture. We had learned from experience with other initiatives that a strong core group in any faculty must own the change before it could transform a school culture. To determine the level of teacher participation (what gets monitored gets done), we stopped collecting detailed data about time usage and started focusing on the number of teachers participating in deep coaching interactions in each school.

> The changes brought about by coaching can be hard to measure in a school that is experiencing many different interventions at once or in which other external issues are causing turmoil. However, if you have limited time and coaching resources, it is important to reflect on the impact it is possible for a coach to have in certain school cultures and place coaches where they will have the deepest and widest impact.

Be Prepared to Face the Challenges and the Treasures

As a child, I watched reruns of an old '60s television program called *Sea Hunt* starring Lloyd Bridges. It was an adventure show about scuba divers who excavated sunken ships that had been lost at sea years before. Divers would go deep below the surface where no light had penetrated for years. When they shone a heavy beam into the hold of the ship, sometimes what they revealed was very scary, and sometimes it was a priceless treasure.

Likewise, when we go deep into a culture of coaching, hidden things, both good and bad, become public. Coaching can shine a light on organizational weaknesses we would prefer to keep hidden and—just as frequently—reveal a sparkling treasure that no one knew existed. Within a short time, you begin to see where your organization's resistance and lack of focus are. Sometimes it might seem easier to turn off the light than to deal with the problem, but if you did that, you would miss the treasure.

Determine What Kinds of Data You Will Collect

As with every step in the process, we begin with our vision and goals for the coaching program, determine our purposes for collecting data, and then decide what kind of information we need to ascertain whether we are meeting our goals. In a classroom, students engage in lessons and assignments every day, but teachers do not grade every learning experience. The same is true with program data collection. We must decide what types of data will get the information to achieve our purposes and avoid collecting piles of data that will never be used. However, it is worthwhile to consider keeping information that perhaps can later be studied in more depth. As with student data, it is important to get a baseline and then decide on intervals for additional monitoring. Ideally, your data collection plan will be well in place by the time your coaches begin their work.

It is very important to be selective about the type and amount of data you ask the coaches to manage. Make sure that the information they must keep is pertinent to the program. We have found through experience if you ask a coach to keep up with a certain kind of activity, he or she may believe it is very important to spend a lot of time doing that activity. For example, you may not want your coaches to spend a lot of time on research, but if you ask them how much time they spend researching, they may interpret your question as a need to do it more frequently.

Guskey (2000) identifies five levels of evaluation for professional learning: participants' reactions, participants' learning, organization support and change, participants' use of new knowledge and skills, and student learning outcomes. As you decide on the kind of data you will collect, it is helpful to keep these five levels in mind and attempt to gather data on all of them. You will want to know how the teachers and principals reacted to coaching, how much they have learned or think they have learned, how much the organization supported the endeavor, how much the teachers and principals used or perceived they used the new learning, and how much student achievement, well-being, confidence, attendance, and performance were impacted.

Of particular interest to us was the level of organization support and change, since our goal was to impact that very culture. Guskey (2000) points out that "Organizational factors at the school and district levels influence what works and what does not work in professional development. In some instances, they can even be defining factors in a program or activity's success" (p. 151). We wanted to gauge the effectiveness of our own support as coaching champions, our district support, and the support of the leaders in the schools in which the coaches worked. Guskey (2000, pp. 152–166) advises asking organizational support questions in the following areas when implementing any professional learning initiative:

- Do organization policies support the endeavor?
- Are appropriate resources provided?
- Is the endeavor protected from intrusion?
- Do members of the organization feel free to experiment without fear?
- Is there collegial support of the endeavor?
- Does the principal support the initiative?
- Do higher level administrators support it?
- Is success recognized?
- Is adequate time provided for the professional learning?

It is informative to develop surveys for or conduct interviews with teachers, coaches, principals, district personnel, and coaching champions to determine the perceived level of support in each of these areas and compare that to the perceived professional learning of the teachers and coaches. This feedback can be very useful and lead to an improvement in administrative support.

Quantitative Data

Quantitative or "countable" data are often persuasive with stakeholders because they use definitive standards and tell a story objectively (Drucker et al., 2008). It is easy to compare things when you have something to "count." This does not mean that quantitative data are any more important, but they are sometimes easier to communicate. It is imperative, in our view, to combine quantitative data with qualitative data in order to understand not only whether your coaching program is working, but why.

According to Bean and Isler (2008), the "gold standard" for showing efficacy is relating coaching directly to student achievement. This is, of course, complex, given the difficulty of controlling for the myriad factors that can affect the achievement of a child. However, it is beneficial to use formative assessments to evaluate the growth of individual students on specific skills after a coach has worked with a teacher in implementing and practicing a new strategy.

Other measures of student growth can also be used—both formal and informal formative assessments can be an integral part of the coaching process, and you might want to require each of your coaches to keep a few of these assessments as artifacts for reflection. Coaches may also keep records of certain student behaviors before and after a specific intervention has been the subject of coaching interactions. For example, you might compare the number of student off-task behaviors before and after a teacher worked with a coach on classroom management techniques. Student test and grade records, student questionnaires, and structured interviews with students can also provide insight into the effect of coaching on student achievement and engagement (Guskey, 2000).

> The kind of research and data collection we are discussing here is "action research" and can have quantitative (number-based) and qualitative (how- and why understanding) elements. With this sort of research, your findings will be applicable primarily to your own setting and cannot be generalized to other settings. While some districts have the resources to conduct sophisticated causal studies, most do not have personnel with the time to take on a large-scale task of this kind. However, local graduate students may wish to pursue this research and share the results with you.

In addition to student data, most coaching programs gather perceptual data from teachers (and administrators) concerning the quality of their work after coaching, and online surveys are a convenient way to do this. The surveys can gather data about teachers' reactions to coaching, their learning, their perception of organization support and change, and their perceived use of new knowledge and skills. Parallel surveys of administrators of these same teachers asking the same sorts of questions can be informative. We chose to conduct systemwide surveys of all teachers at the end of each year concerning coaching relationships and effects.

There are many good resources about how to design a good survey. In general, the questions should be structured and clear, and the instructions should state the purpose of the survey and how the responses will be used. Since we were looking for opinions, perceptions, and attitudes, most of our questions were *rating* questions, with a scale of 1 to 5 or 1 to 7. It is a good idea to include one open-ended question to allow respondents to give specific information or ideas. We avoided asking questions that might identify a respondent and only asked personal information that might assist us in improving our program, such as the years of experience, teaching grade level, or subject. We feel it is always important to ask the number, focus, and type of coach–teacher interactions that the teacher has experienced. It is a good idea to select an online survey system that allows you to filter responses based on the answer to one or more specific responses to a question. This makes it possible to filter the answers based on one response, such as teachers who had two or fewer coaching experiences and those who had three or more coaching experiences. Filtering for the amount of time a coach is assigned to a school can also help you see whether lack of time may account for differences in responses.

To make your survey more useful, you can also filter your answers based on grade level taught. You might have noticed that high school teachers in your district have fewer coaching experiences than do elementary teachers and wonder why that is so. You might formulate several hypotheses, such as a lower trust level or a limited amount of time to collaborate at the high school level. You can then filter on the high school teachers' perceptions of trust in the coach and on their perceived amount of time to work with the coach. Perhaps you find that most high school teachers who did not work frequently with a coach had a low level of trust in their coach. That information can focus the coaches' efforts on building trust at the secondary level, while at another grade level other issues— such as time available for coaching—might be a greater hindrance to coaching.

If you are a district-level champion, principals are excellent sources of important information concerning the effectiveness of the coaches and the program in general. Consider the size of your system when determining whether it is more effective to survey or interview your principals. We found it informative to survey principals about coaching twice a year. Some small systems with few administrators may wish to conduct only interviews with principals. An added benefit of a survey is that it reminds principals of some of the activities they were to be doing with their coaches, such as meeting with them regularly and encouraging their teachers to participate in coaching activities or professional learning communities. If you are a principal championing a coach in your own school, conduct a self-assessment of your interactions with your coach and hold reflective conversations with any other leaders in the building.

Qualitative Data

It is always satisfying to be able to count the numbers of coaching interactions or calculate the amount of time spent on important district initiatives, but often some of the richest information about coaching comes from qualitative methods—the study of the depth and intricacies of coaching and teaching interactions. According to Drucker and colleagues (2008), "These two types of measures are interwoven—they shed light on one another—and both are necessary to illuminate in what ways lives are being changed" (pp. 52–53).

Observations: Summative data concerning the observation of certain teacher practices before and after coaching can also paint a picture of the efficacy of the program. Administrators and instructional supervisors take notes of a teacher's specific instructional or classroom management practice and compare its effectiveness before and after coaching. For these kinds of data to be meaningful, the observers must be very focused and write about what they expect to see before they see it and then compare their expectations with their observations.

Videotaping: This is an easy way to observe and share observations. Small and convenient video cameras (such as Flip cameras) are required equipment for the coaching toolkit. While we feel all teachers should videotape their teaching in order for them to reflect on their own practice, it is also helpful to videotape coaches interacting with the people they coach. We required each of our coaches to videotape a pre- and postconference with a teacher and then review it with a peer coach to discuss areas of potential improvement. We did not require that this be shared with anyone in an administrative role, as our purpose was for individual coach reflection. We did ask, however, that they videotape themselves at regular intervals, watch and compare the interactions over time, reflect on ways that they had grown and intended to grow in the future, and share these reflections.

Personal reflections: At regular intervals, we asked coaches, principals, and teachers to reflect on what personal experiences they had with coaching. The results were moving and very enlightening.

The voices of the coaches and administrators were stronger and more focused over time. These reflections should be captured in a variety of ways: through written reflections, focus group discussions, comments on surveys, and videotaped interviews. A benefit of asking for personal reflections in the comment section of an online survey is that the comments could be filtered based on demographics or the answers to certain questions. For example, you could select all the comments made by teachers at a certain grade level or with a certain number of years of experience. Sometimes interesting patterns emerged when looking at the perceived experiences of new teachers as compared to veteran teachers who participated in coaching.

Regular coaching meetings are good times for coaches to share their reflections and to ask for additional program and peer support. Our regular "Friday Focus" meetings include a component of responsiveness to coach concerns. The coaches submit their questions or concerns on Thursday for anonymous inclusion on the Friday agenda. (See Chapter 3 resources section for a sample Friday Focus form.)

Portfolios: It is important to keep a history of your coaching program. One of the most convenient ways to do this is to have coaches keep a coaching portfolio. This can be done electronically in what our coaches called an "e-portfolio." All of the artifacts of the coach's year were kept on a thumb drive—videos of conferences, photos of student work galleries, audiovisual presentations, newsletters—and shared at the end of the year. Some coaches put together videos, PechaKucha, Prezi, or PowerPoint presentations identifying the highlights of their coaching experiences. This information is excellent to share and promotes collaboration among coaches. It also demonstrates to the coach and other stakeholders the large amount of work coaches do in the course of a year. See Chapter 3 resources for a sample description of e-portfolio requirements.

REFLECT   Consider your goals for coaches, coaching champions, administrators, and students. Brainstorm two or three types of data for each group that will reflect progress toward these goals.

Evaluate and Communicate the Results

We don't always make an A on every test. Sometimes we don't lose 10 pounds after a month on a diet. Frequently, the data do not tell us what we want to see—and they really don't tell us what we want to tell other people! But hopefully they tell us what is true. The challenge is communicating that information to the people who need to know it in an honest yet kind way. We all have a tendency to focus on the negative in a message, no matter how positive the results are. We also know that sometimes while acknowledging effort, we must also point out challenges that need to be addressed explicitly. Data are an excellent tool to accomplish both of these goals.

Our experience has been that coaches (and teachers) take data about their work extremely personally. That is a good thing, because it means they care passionately about the work. It also means that we have to exercise sensitivity in revealing information. I recall a subject area team meeting years ago in which the principal handed out everyone's student achievement test results. One teacher immediately noticed her students had the lowest scores, and her eyes filled with tears. Although student achievement data are not intended to be competitive, in a culture of isolation, it can seem that way. This is a caution for those of us who work in cultures that are not yet collaborative and collegial. Sometimes you must share specific and negative data with a particular coach. This requires the fierce conversations of honesty that can be uncomfortable but productive. Scott, in the book *Fierce Conversations* (2004), discusses the negative emotional wake caused by our words. This wake can be minimized by being intentional and choosing words that are not emotionally charged.

When the data are in, it is time to evaluate them. Data are raw material, and evaluation is the process of looking at that raw material and drawing something valuable and helpful from it. It is a good idea to get input from a variety of stakeholders to help make sense of the data that you collect. Coaches themselves are the first people who can help you interpret the data's meaning.

Share Assessment Results With Coaches, Teachers, or Administrators

- Distribute coaching survey findings and have each stakeholder (principal, coach, district supervisor) review and mark findings that were surprising, disappointing, and exciting. After they have time to make those decisions, have them move to groups of four or five and share their reactions. Alternately, the findings can be posted on chart paper and individuals can do a "data walk" around the room, marking the most significant results (in their opinion) with a colored dot sticker. Discuss the findings as a larger group. What does the information indicate? What actions could we take to get a more satisfying result?

- Take data from coaching interaction tally forms and create three types of charts of summary data: the individual coaches' data, the grade and/or subject group data, and the district data. Have coaches review the chart of the district data and anticipate where they personally would fall on the chart. Then divide the participants into grade or subject groups and distribute the grade or subject group summary data (elementary, middle, and high or math, reading, English, etc.) and have the grade group coaches meet and chart where their data fell in comparison to other grade groups and/or subject groups. Finally, distribute individual data. Have coaches review it privately and reflect on where they fall on the chart and why. This same exercise can be done with principals to reveal their school-level data and to give them time to reflect on how their school culture is embracing coaching.

- Use Pip Wilson's "Blob Tree" (n.d.) to assess where coaches feel they are in the coaching process. (The "Blob Tree" is a picture of a tree with many bloblike individuals interacting with the tree on various levels—from climbing it to falling off of it to sitting beneath it. It is a good way to start a conversation about how an individual feels about almost any situation. The participants in the conversation start by identifying themselves with one of the blobs and then describing why that blob might represent them.) Coaches have also used this technique with teachers, and it could be equally effective with principals or district personnel. You can purchase a poster-size Blob Tree to put on the wall and ask coaches to mark the figure that most reflects their position in the coaching process by placing a colored dot sticker on the tree. They can use a different-colored dot to indicate where they were at some point in the past or where they would like to be by some point in the future. This is an excellent exercise to open up self-reflective dialog.

Frequently it is necessary to distribute data results to larger groups of stakeholders in a large meeting or even newsletter form. In these cases, it is important to emphasize the formative nature of the assessments. It can be effective to use a bar or pie chart with the end goal and the current data as portions of that long-term goal. That encourages all stakeholders to see change as a process.

> *"IF IT IS WORTH LEARNING, IT IS WORTH CELEBRATING! Celebration provides feedback regarding progress and increases positive emotion associations with the learning."*
>
> —Bobbi DePorter (n.d.)

Celebrate Success

Every day, millions of small interactions between people occur that lay the groundwork for more intentional, reflective teaching and learning. Too seldom do we celebrate these daily miracles! Brain-based learning research shows that student motivation to learn is increased when effort is acknowledged. It is no different for adult learners—teachers and coaches.

Celebration and shared history build community. We used Friday Focus forms to gather these items of celebration and then incorporated them into regular coaching meetings. The forms also served as a history of good things that occurred in the program. Coaches used their video cameras to capture exciting highlights of the month and shared them at meetings. At the end of the year, one coach developed a humorous retrospective of the trials and tribulations of beginning coaches. Many coaching programs also make effective use of coaching e-mail lists that announce successes and share information among coaches. Coaching blogs and wikis serve a similar purpose of communal celebration as well as their primary purpose of sharing information.

Celebration is mutually beneficial motivation. Modeling celebration with the coaching group leads to greater celebration in the schools by the coaches and teachers. After a coach celebration, they take many of the celebration rituals back to the schools. Several high school coaches developed a video of students thanking their teachers for what they had done for them. They then showed the video at the end-of-year faculty meeting. There wasn't a dry eye in the group as they watched a big tough football player talk about how his English teacher changed his life and an ESL student thank her science teacher for giving her extra help so she could do well enough on the ACT to go to college! Coaches also create and send weekly news—e-mails and electronic newsletters to administrators and teachers to announce noteworthy events. These mini celebrations foster a culture of gratefulness and positive energy in a school and in a coaching program. The main purpose of celebration is to acknowledge the value of the work we do.

Summary

Steps to a coaching program assessment plan:

1. Set program goals and coaching goals.

2. Determine the purposes of your assessment.

3. Determine what information will meet your purposes and support your goals.

4. Acknowledge factors that may be beyond your control.

5. Prepare to see the problems as well as the treasures.

6. Choose your assessments.

7. Reflect on the data and communicate your results.

8. Consider how you can refine your program based on the data.

9. Celebrate your successes!

We must keep our eyes on the data, our arms around good systems to collect and review it, and our hearts tender for students, teachers, and coaches to prepare our coaching program for the unexpected.

Building an Instructional Coaching Program for Maximum Capacity

1. Research coaching and coaching models. Reach out to others (coaches, coaching champions) in the professional community. (Chapter 1)

2. Select a "champion team" who will develop the coaching initiative and will support coaching. (Chapter 2)

3. Develop a shared vision of instructional coaching for your school or district. (Chapter 2)

4. Align your vision of instructional coaching with your school or district's vision. (Chapter 2)

5. Develop an administrative model for coaching. (Chapter 2)

6. Develop your assessment plan for the coaching initiative. Know what you will evaluate and how you will do it. (Chapter 3)

7. **Know the five characteristics of great coaches prior to hiring and assigning, and use them to develop a recruitment strategy. Interview and hire coaches. (Chapter 4)**

8. Determine preservice training needs for administrators and supervisors and develop a learning plan. (Chapter 5)

9. Determine preservice training needs for newly hired instructional coaches and develop a learning plan for the first of the school year as part of a long-term comprehensive model of ongoing professional learning and support. (Chapter 6)

10. Plan for opportunities for regular collaboration among and between coaches and teachers after coaches begin. (Chapter 7)

11. Develop a model of ongoing learning and support for instructional coaches. (Chapter 8)

12. Evaluate your coaching program and make necessary adjustments to sustain, change, abandon, or reimagine your coaching initiative. (Chapters 3 and 9)

4

Ready, Set, Sail

Selecting the Coaching Crew

When the school system "fleet" sets sail on a new school year, all the crew must be willing and ready for the challenge, but the coach, who is the "model teacher," must be the right crewman for that vessel and that voyage. To modify a metaphor from the bestselling book *Good to Great* (Collins, 2001), the captain must get the wrong people off the ship, get the right people on the ship, and get everyone in the right places on the ship. This must be done intentionally and thoughtfully before you can even decide the path of the ship.

> *"More than learning a few dozen skills and techniques, success in coaching can hinge on first developing a deep understanding of people and transformation."*
>
> —Karla Reiss (2009, p. 180)

Apply Your Coaching Administrative Model to Your Hiring Plan

In Chapter 2, we discussed the key decisions you must make when developing a coaching program. Now it is important to revisit seven of the decisions you made in the following areas as you make related decisions about the coach selection process:

1. What are the goals of your coaching program?

2. What is the role of a coach in your coaching program?

3. Will the coaches work for one school or for the district? If the district, how many schools will they serve?

4. Who will supervise the coaches? Who will participate in hiring?

5. How will your coaches be matched with their schools?

6. Who will champion the coaches?

7. What rules will control the hiring, placement, and evaluation of coaches?

This information from your administrative model will impact the most important decision you will make: who your coaches will be. With answers to these questions in place, you can move to the next phase in your program implementation—seeking and hiring the right coaches.

The first decision—**defining the goals**—will drive the sorts of specific skill sets you will look for in a coach. Often we set program goals but don't force ourselves to face those goals in every staffing decision, and sometimes this leads to placing good people in the wrong jobs. Your program goals are paramount and should be (literally) in front of you every step of the way. We suggest a "bottom-line question." Using your goal, create a question that you will come back to again and again as you make personnel selections. For example,

"Can (insert name), as a coach, teach our teachers to be more reflective and collaborative professionals, focusing on student learning?"

"Can (insert name), as a coach, disseminate the district initiative of greater student engagement in high school math classrooms?"

As you can see, a good coach may not be able to help you meet both of those goals. If he or she can do only one, this is not the person you need for that position. One Florida principal who implemented coaching in her school wanted to do two things—help teachers be more responsive to the needs of a high-poverty population and implement a new math program. She divided her applicants into three categories—those with experience in high-poverty environments, those with experience implementing new math programs, and those with both. From the third pile, she began her interview process.

The second decision, **defining the role of the coaches** in your coaching program, should be revisited at this time. With this definition in hand, you will be able to create the job description that will advertise your coaching positions. Please be aware that coaches are called by different names in various states, and in some areas, people may be unfamiliar with the concept. Your job posting will need to briefly describe your approach to coaching and include the role of coaches in your district. Before creating this posting, you may wish to review the example posting in the Chapter 4 resources section, but remember that each one will be unique, as the nature of the job is unique. The job posting must fit the goals and objectives identified by your leadership team, and it must conform to all local guidelines. Perhaps you want the coach to help your teachers with formative assessments or technology implementation or a host of other specific district initiatives. Expertise required to fill these roles must be delineated in your job posting. Additionally, your state may offer an endorsement certificate for coaches; this is something you will need to discover as you develop your job posting.

Are you beginning a coaching initiative as a single school, or are you part of a larger district that is implementing coaching? If you are in a larger district or diocese, the third decision, the **number of schools each coach will be assigned,** is usually an economic one.

How many can we afford? But the answer—one per school, one per department, one per district—can affect the qualities of the person you want to hire. Obviously, if the person will travel to many schools, she or he must have a level of organization, energy, and flexibility that a one-school or one-department coach may not require. This person may need to be willing to travel long distances between schools and be a "nomad" with his or her workspace. The traveling coach will have to develop a rotating schedule of work. This information must also be included in the job posting.

I had the experience of starting a new preschool program in a remote rural location. I needed an excellent pre-K teacher, and I had the problem we would all love to have—too many excellent applicants! After we sifted through the pile of applications and selected our interviewees, we found ourselves faced with eight bright, enthusiastic, personable, and knowledgeable teachers! How then to decide? This particular job assignment had one negative—it was not located in the regular school building close to the principal, mentors, and coworkers. It was 5 minutes away in a building that would essentially be "managed" by the teacher. So, then, on top of the other qualities needed in a pre-K teacher, I had to ask myself the following questions: (1) *Which candidate would be able to maintain enthusiasm and direction absent localized supervision and support?* and (2) *Which candidate would be most likely to be able to manage a building and personnel should a problem arise before an administrator could arrive?* When we asked and answered these questions, one person from the group of applicants came immediately to mind, and she was hired.

Sometimes the particular circumstances of a situation can drastically affect the hiring and placement process: You will have to ask yourself if the coach will work best with a very new faculty or with a more seasoned one. Will the coach's experience and personality be best suited to an academic magnet school or an alternative school for children who have had discipline issues? You will have to probe the prejudices and comfort level of teaching different subjects—will the coach be too biased against, for example, science instruction because it was his or her least favorite subject?

The fourth decision, **who will supervise the coaches,** is also important to the hiring process because it will help your leadership team decide who needs to be involved in the selection process. Will the principal or a district-level employee be the direct supervisor? Will you adopt a hybrid "facilitator" model, in which the principal supervises and the district personnel manage the program but not the people? Generally, it is more difficult for coaches to be viewed by teachers as "one of us" if they are supervised by district personnel. However, if you have a multischool schedule, you have no alternative. If you are using a district-supervised model or a facilitator model, it will be even more important that the coach's demeanor is one of "personal humility" in combination with "professional will" (Collins, 2001).

After you decide to whom the coach will be accountable, you will have a good idea of how to form your coach search team. The potential supervisor (school or district level) along with any key curriculum personnel should participate. Even if the supervisor is a district person, you should include representative principals on your team. If the coach is a subject area expert—literacy coach or math coach, for example—then the appropriate curricular supervisors or lead teachers should be involved. Some districts hire "pools" of coaches, and then school teams choose who they prefer for their school. No matter who is on your selection team, you must take the time to have a shared understanding of the desired roles and qualities of a coach in your program prior to the beginning of the selection process.

The fifth decision, **how coaches will be matched to schools**, will impact the background you seek in the coaching candidate. If you have a 1:1 (one-coach/one-school) model, you will need to have some conversation about whether to seek out a candidate from within that school. Frequently this works well, because the coach already has a rapport with the teachers and staff and has knowledge of the culture of the school. Of course, it can be difficult to make the role transition for some people, especially if the coach is perceived to be the "favorite" of administration. Trust issues and questions of whether the coach is actually an "administrative spy" can come up in any model, and this is something to consider carefully. In a 1:1 model, it may be the principal who makes the final hiring decision, whether or not he or she chooses from among current faculty or from a pool that has already been vetted by a district selection team. In either case, what works best to assuage trust anxieties is to involve teachers in the selection process.

You have already determined who your coaching champions are. If you have a large district and many coaches, you will need to identify **which coaches will work with which champion.** This relationship is important and could influence the balance or the congruence you wish to achieve.

Finally, make sure you **understand the policies, rules, and laws** surrounding the hiring of coaches. Applicants will want to know answers about tenure, evaluation, promotion, and rank within your school or district and how those will be applied to their new position.

Know What You Want in a Coach

Collins (2001) identifies five basic characteristics of the "right" people in organizations in his book *Good to Great*. These people share the core values of the organization; they are not people you need to manage, they are the best in their current position; they understand the difference between having a job and holding a responsibility; and they are the kind of people you would hire again if you had the chance. In coaching, many of these same principles apply. For our purposes, we modified Collins's five characteristics and added an indispensible sixth that must be present in a good coach to create a list of imperative qualities of coaches (IQCs).

When starting a new coaching program, it is important that the coach selection team be in accord about the kind of applicant they are seeking. It is time well spent to go through a group reflective process so that everyone involved shares a vision of the type of person who will carry out this very important role—because without the right crew, the ship will not sail. If time permits, you may wish to conduct a book study with your selection team of Collins's *Good to Great* (2001).

The selection team must consider the imperative qualities of coaches outlined below and come to consensus about what each looks like and sounds like to them and to their educational setting. The quality coach is

- visionary,
- courageous,
- a masterful teacher,
- balanced,
- treasured, and
- a person of arête.

The Coach Must Be a Visionary

When people take great personal and professional risks, they must believe in the mission and have a vision of the future. The coach must model an inspirational attitude and be one of the greatest ambassadors of your organization's values. But to do this, the coach's own values must align with the values of the organization. It cannot be false or fake. In general, a coach must value learning and be passionate about professional growth. The coach must have a strong sense that student achievement is the overriding goal of any school and must believe that the job of the professional educator is to leave no stone unturned in the pursuit of educational experiences that will foster student learning. Finally, a coach must be willing to embrace the vision of the school and district and to carry it out. Sometimes this means the coach has a long history and familiarity with the school or district, but often an outsider can have an even clearer perspective of the organization's goals.

Some questions that might reveal a visionary include the following:

- Describe the mission and vision of your current school or district. How do you see your role in living out that mission in the organization?
- Share your vision of the future of education.
- How do your own personal values affect your role as a teacher leader?
- Describe one of the most meaningful professional development experiences you have had. How did it impact your practice?

The Coach Must Be Courageous

Sometimes we think of courage in terms of doing battle, but the kind of courage a coach needs is the ability to do the job, day in and day out, without the fear of failure or inadequacy. A school or district must provide a coach with support, professional learning opportunities, feedback, and encouragement, but you do not need someone who must continually be stroked, checked up on, or monitored. You might want to think twice if a reference includes the statement "She is an excellent teacher when given a specific direction." More than likely, this is not a coach. A coach can be given a vision and a mission and can carry it out even when it means risking being liked. All new coaches will have some trepidation, but they must be willing to put aside their insecurities for the good of the students. One coach with whom we worked expressed it like this: "A coach needs to have a strong sense of self. It can be a lonely position. There will be times when you will be rejected. You will have to do some tough stuff and take risks, but it is easier to do when you know that it is for the kids that you are doing it."

Coaches must be courageous enough to forge their own path while they play with the team. A coach must have holonomy—the ability to be self-directed and to be a team player at the same time (Costa & Garmston, 2002). Coaches may have a different job description in every building they go into, and this job description is often one that they must create themselves in collaboration with their supervisors. Some individuals require more concrete direction and supervision than others, and sometimes these people make great coaches when paired with principals with a certain administrative style. However, in general, you want to hire someone who can handle shifting job responsibilities while maintaining both autonomy and collegiality.

Some questions that might reveal workplace courage include the following:

- Describe a time when you were given a large and complex task to complete. How did you tackle it?
- Describe the best supervisor you have had. What made him or her stand out from among the rest?
- What kinds of management styles or techniques do you find empowering and exciting?
- If you were given a large job with a short amount of time to complete it, would you prefer to work with a team or on your own? Why?
- Have you been given a task and told to work with a group of adults who did not want to work with you? If so, what did you do to make sure the task was completed?

The Coach Must Be a Masterful Teacher

Coaches are, at heart, always teachers. They must never lose that perspective. In their new roles, they are still teaching students, but doing so by developing the skills and promoting the reflective thinking of everyone in a school. Knight (2004) states "at their core, coaches need to continually communicate their deep, honest belief in teachers, even when they also are communicating specific ways in which teachers need to improve their teaching practices" (p. 3). This is the same statement that could be made of teachers: They must continually communicate their deep, honest belief in students, even when they also are communicating specific ways in which the students need to improve.

Coaches need to have exceptional teaching skills and be recognized by their peers as among the best already. For us, that meant that no matter how good they were, they needed to be seasoned and have at least 5 years of *exemplary* experience. In cases where a teacher has a rocky start to her career, that experience time needs to be even longer.

At a national conference, I sat next to a young woman named Cindy who shared with me that she discovered on the first day of her work as a coach that the teacher who had supervised her student teaching 8 years before in another district was on that staff. Cindy had been 22, not too ambitious, and enjoying the social life of college more than the academic—hardly an unusual story. Her student teaching experience had not been a good one, and even though Cindy went on to become an exemplary teacher and coach by the time she was 30, the impression the supervising teacher had of her was still her 22-year-old inexperienced self. It was very difficult for the coach to overcome this early impression with that teacher and the others on the faculty who listened to her, so Cindy finally went to the teacher and said, "I want you to know that I have grown a lot in the last 8 years, partially because of lessons you taught me. I'd like for you to see me teach again and look at how far I have come with the help of my colleagues and coaches! If I can improve this much, think how much coaching can change a faculty!" The teacher did, and they forged a positive working relationship as colleagues. This negative, with the right attitude of humility, was transformed into a positive.

Research shows that effective coaches must have, in addition to interpersonal skills, an exceptional grasp of the content and of the pedagogy for that content. We found that a master's degree was an important qualification in most cases. It indicated to us that the teacher wanted to go above and beyond minimum requirements and that he or she had ambitious career goals. Even if the graduate degree was not directly related to the coaching job, it showed a dedication and ability to complete high-level tasks. Some degrees that we found helpful were, of course, content area degrees (math, science, reading specialist, special education, English language learning, etc.), as well as administration, supervision, communication, and curriculum.

In addition to the educational background, a strong commitment to ongoing professional learning must be evident. The experience of working in and perhaps leading a professional learning community is important, and the experience of having been coached themselves is *lagniappe*! Coaches should have a positive and realistic view of adult learning styles, and it is helpful if they have had experience leading or teaching adults in a group setting. Knight (2004) says,

"Simply put, no matter how much coaches know, they won't win over teachers unless they can be successful in the classroom" (p. 3).

Some questions that might reveal a masterful teacher include the following:

- Describe a recent lesson you have taught. What were the students doing? What would you wish to improve next time?
- Pretend I walked into your classroom unannounced on a Wednesday morning. What might I see?
- There are many different instructional models, from direct instruction to problem-based or inquiry learning. What are some different models you have used successfully in the classroom?
- What do you do in your classroom to make sure you meet the needs of diverse learners?
- If we asked you to teach a lesson on _____ to a group of students you did not know, what would you do to prepare? How would you approach the lesson?

Many schools and districts require applicants to conduct a model lesson or submit a brief lesson on videotape as a part of the application process. This is especially vital when hiring a teacher from outside the school or district. We also found that a written statement is very revealing of the six traits we were looking for, in addition to revealing the ability to communicate well and clearly in writing.

The Coach Must Be Balanced

Sailors talk of "getting their sea legs." That sense of physical balance you must maintain while sailing can be compared to the emotional balance you must have as a coach. Coaches are people who seek ways to fulfill every role to the best of their ability, but they understand that those roles must be carefully balanced. They cannot take on a backpack with all the cares and responsibilities of an entire faculty and still be able to stand upright, but at the same time, they cannot expect others to hold them up all the time.

Good coaches are aware that their job has broadened and deepened. Coaching is a hybrid job—you are a teacher, possibly earning teacher pay for your coaching, but you are now responsible for the achievement of *many* students and perhaps even held accountable by many administrators. The coach is responsible for the success of the educational organization as a whole. Hours might be longer and less predictable, and the coach will likely have less control over his or her schedule: A teacher may decide to give a test that is quickly graded or one that will require more time to grade, but coaches may not have this flexibility as they strive to meet the goals of the school or district at large—often on someone else's timetable. Travel to conferences and professional development activities may be involved and take up family time and weekends. The coach must have physical and emotional stamina and be able to maintain balance and perspective in the role. They are what Collins (2001) described as "productively neurotic."

Some interview questions that might reveal balance include the following:

- We all have challenges in balancing work and personal responsibilities. What are some ways you have handled these challenges in the past?
- What are some ways that you use your personal experiences to enrich your professional life?
- Coaching requires unpredictable hours and occasional travel. How do you envision yourself making the adjustment to a schedule that does not always conform to the school-year calendar?
- Teaching and coaching require a lot of time-management skills. What methods do you use to keep on top of all the tasks that you must complete in your current job?
- Describe a time when you have been under extreme professional or personal stress. What strategies did you use to respond to this challenge?

The Coach Must Be a Treasure

I've never used a metal detector, but I've been impacted by one—a number of years ago an amateur "treasure hunter" found my father's college ring on a beach in Florida—many years after and many hundreds of miles from where it had been lost. The beachcomber called the university, got the alumni list from the year on the ring, and began calling all the men in that class until he found the person who had lost his ring—as it turned out, my father. He realized he had found someone's treasure, and he took it seriously. Collins (2001) says the "right person" in your organization is someone you would hire again if you had a chance. We think it goes even farther than that. It is someone that you value so much that your organization would be truly diminished without her—a treasure.

We have all had employees who are treasures—you just hope the day never comes when they leave your organization, and you will do anything you can to keep them. In determining a treasure, prior employer references are very important. A direct phone call with a prior employer before you make the decision to hire is very important. Sometimes this is a painful process, because as you are asking for a reference, you are also asking the prior supervisor to let this employee go.

In interviews, you discover some people who are running *to* a greater opportunity and others who are running *from* a bad experience. Treasures are people who leave good experiences and feelings wherever they go, and when they must leave, it is because a deeper and richer opportunity awaits. The slightest suggestion that this person "wants out of the classroom" or "didn't see eye to eye with administration" should cause you to think twice. That person might be running from instead of toward something. You are looking for that person who adds value and richness.

Some interview questions that might reveal treasures include the following:

- What do you think your most important contributions to your current school or district have been?
- How would your current principal or supervisor describe you?
- How would your colleagues describe you?
- What would be the most difficult thing about leaving your current job?
- What kind of contribution do you think you can make to our school or district?

Some reference questions that might reveal this include the following:

- When you were supervising (coach applicant's name), how would you describe your day-to-day working relationship?
- If (coach applicant's name) decides to take another position, what will you or your organization miss the most?

The Coach Must Be a Person of Arête

Arête is a Greek word used to refer to excellence and living up to your full potential. It was the point of the Greek *paideia*, or training of a boy to manhood. Aristotle argued that arête could not really be defined, because each being or object has a different purpose to achieve. In our view, a coach must have arête—he or she must live up to his or her potential and be willing to take the difficult path with grace and wit.

In the *Odyssey*, Homer frequently equated arête with prowess in the battlefield, but Odysseus's wife Penelope's arête of cooperation and faithfulness was also praised. A coach must be tough and strong yet loyal and faithful. The Greeks illustrated this concept by personifying

Arête as the sister of Harmony and the daughter of Justice. Indeed, the best coaches I have known have a keen sense of both: They can walk in harmony but act justly. In the ancient Old Testament Bible, the prophet Micah defined the concept of arête as "to do justly, and to love mercy, and to walk humbly" (King James Version).

Collins (2001) described a *Level 5* leader as one who combines personal humility and professional will. This is what the best coaches are. They are ambitious—but for their work and their students, not for themselves. They push for tough and difficult causes, but they maintain a positive and cheerful demeanor. They are willing to give up some personal good will if it means saying something unpopular that must be said to provide a student the best possible learning experience. In a word, the best coaches have arête, a quality that takes a lifetime to acquire. Coaches themselves ranked their interpersonal skills of greater importance than content or pedagogical knowledge—they believed the people skills are more difficult to acquire (Kowal & Steiner, 2007).

Knight (2004) described this quality of will and humility this way:

> Instructional coaches are more effective if they have what we have come to call an "infectious personality." Instructional coaches need to have energy and a positive outlook, and they need to be the kind of person others enjoy being around. Coaches need to be, as one coach has commented, "respectfully pushy." (p. 3)

One high school coach summed it up this way: "The most important quality a coach can have is a desire to learn and an awareness of how much you don't know." An elementary coach from the same district concurred: "Coaches should be smart and friendly. They must be adept at speaking to many different types of personalities and groups of people . . . it helps to be humble yet confident, easy to get along with, and helpful."

I was traveling on a plane recently to visit my newborn nephew in California. I was looking forward to reading my book, taking a nap, and starting my weeklong vacation after a very busy year. For those of you who travel a lot, you will understand that I was concerned when the passenger next to me immediately engaged me in conversation—at the *beginning* of a 5-hour flight!

Less than 2 minutes into the conversation, I discovered she was an instructional coach in North Carolina. Intrigued, I asked her how she got into the field of instructional coaching.

She smiled and told her story: "Eight years ago, I didn't even know what an instructional coach was! I was relocating to North Carolina, and I went to a job interview for a teaching position.

Halfway through the interview, the principal said, 'Would you accept a position as an instructional coach? You have just the personality for it!' I hesitated—I wasn't sure what the job was, but I knew I needed to work, so I said, 'Sure!' I thought I would give it a try for a year and see what it is all about—and I never turned back! It has been the best thing that has ever happened to me professionally!"

I saw what I am sure her principal saw: a person who had a sense of arête. She asked questions, she listened, she offered her own ideas in an engaging and humble way, and her eyes shone when she mentioned her students, her teachers, her principal. She was the type of person you really wouldn't mind talking to for 5 hours, but she was perceptive enough to wind down the conversation after about 45 minutes!

Some interview questions that might reveal arête include the following:

- Tell me about something in which you believe passionately.
- If you could change anything about education today, what would it be?
- Describe your greatest strength and your greatest weakness.
- If a student tells you about a serious problem he is having with another teacher, how would you handle it? Would you handle it differently if a colleague came to you with such a problem?
- Think of the biggest professional challenge you have experienced. How did you handle it? Would you handle it differently if you had it to do over?

REFLECT: As you read through the imperative qualities of coaches and the sample questions that follow them, develop one or two additional questions that might help determine whether the candidate possesses the described characteristic.

Visionary, courageous, masterful, balanced, treasured, arête . . . Reading over the imperative qualities of coaches, you may despair that you will ever find this perfect person (and if you do, you may want to marry him or her). But one of the miracles of coaching is there actually are people like this out there, and if they have not completely met their potential yet, with the right team, encouragement, and support, they can become who they need to be.

Summary: Wrapping Up the Hiring Process

1. Review your organization's program goals and decisions and reflect on how they will impact your selection team's composition and procedures.

2. Finalize the composition of the selection committee. If practical, invite stakeholders to submit a "looks like/sounds like" exercise to the committee.

3. Make sure your selection team knows what they, as a team, are looking for in a coach.

4. Review the imperative qualities of coaches (IQCs) and develop appropriate interview questions and job application requirements.

5. Create a job posting with a description and applicant requirements.

6. Advertise the position via regular hiring channels in your district, making sure you have followed all policies, procedures, and contractual obligations.

7. Rate resumes and application packets, using a team approach if possible. Select the candidates you wish to interview using a check sheet of requirements or a rubric.

8. Handle all interviews in the same manner—the same questions, in the same order. Use a rubric to rate the interviewees' answers.

9. Make the selection process transparent so that all personnel understand this was a group decision—the coach is not the "darling" of the school or district leader.

As you launch your coaching venture, you are expanding the horizons of the captain and crew—administrators and staff—of what it means to be a professional teacher leader. Keep this in mind as you progress through the sometimes difficult process of implementation. Teachers will reap the rewards of your efforts as they experience the freedom that comes from opening their classroom doors and making their practice, both the challenges and victories, public.

Building an Instructional Coaching Program for Maximum Capacity

1. Research coaching and coaching models. Reach out to others (coaches, coaching champions) in the professional community. (Chapter 1)

2. Select a "champion team" who will develop the coaching initiative and will support coaching. (Chapter 2)

3. Develop a shared vision of instructional coaching for your school or district. (Chapter 2)

4. Align your vision of instructional coaching with your school or district's vision. (Chapter 2)

5. Develop an administrative model for coaching. (Chapter 2)

6. Develop your assessment plan for the coaching initiative. Know what you will evaluate and how you will do it. (Chapter 3)

7. Know the five characteristics of great coaches prior to hiring and assigning, and use them to develop a recruitment strategy. Interview and hire coaches. (Chapter 4)

8. **Determine preservice training needs for administrators and supervisors and develop a learning plan. (Chapter 5)**

9. Determine preservice training needs for newly hired instructional coaches and develop a learning plan for the first of the school year as part of a long-term comprehensive model of ongoing professional learning and support. (Chapter 6)

10. Plan for opportunities for regular collaboration among and between coaches and teachers after coaches begin. (Chapter 7)

11. Develop a model of ongoing learning and support for instructional coaches. (Chapter 8)

12. Evaluate your coaching program and make necessary adjustments to sustain, change, abandon, or reimagine your coaching initiative. (Chapters 3 and 9)

5

O, Captain, My Captain

Preparing the Principal

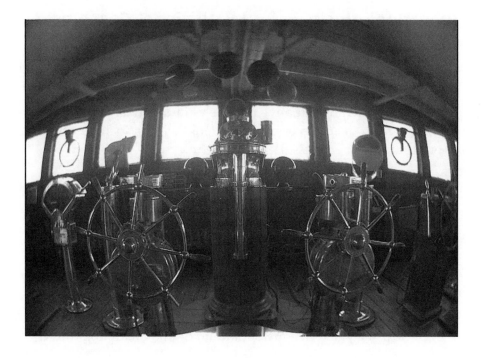

When implementing a successful coaching program, the most important role is that of the principal. As Killion and Harrison (2006) point out, "principals have a significant responsibility for providing coaches with the necessary support" (p. 115). Additionally, the principal sets the course for any school initiative. Therefore, a well-developed professional learning program for principals must be in place even before instructional coaches are hired. The professional learning principals receive will focus on helping them understand what instructional coaching is, why it is a viable professional learning model, how instructional coaching can support teachers in their day-to-day practice, and what the roles and responsibilities of the principal are in fostering the success of the coaching program.

Many times, principals or teacher leader teams embark on a coaching program without the benefit of district support. If this is the case, it is even more vital that you seek the professional learning mentioned in this chapter from some source. You may wish to consider partnering with other principals or teacher leaders in other districts or schools to gain your professional learning.

Preparing Principals for Instructional Coaching

When preparing to introduce principals to instructional coaching, you may find it helpful to use a backward design, similar to the design you learned about in Chapter 2. Your plan for orienting principals to the coaching initiative may be as in-depth as you and your champion team deem necessary but should at least include learning opportunities that address the following topics:

1. Leading a change initiative

2. How instructional coaching supports and facilitates change

3. The role of the instructional coach

4. The role of the principal

5. The role of the coaching champion

6. Communication among stakeholders

7. The principal–coach memorandum of understanding (MOU)

Leading a Change Initiative

Enduring change in any organization requires the momentum that comes from developing a collective mind-set and capacity for the desired change. To develop such collective mind-sets, principals must understand on a deep level the implications of the learning–leading connection (Lambert, 2003) as they assume their roles as agents of change. Principals as lead learners build capacity—both individual and collective—in their schools, and capacity is essential for sustaining a change initiative.

In simplest terms, capacity reveals itself in individuals who perform at their highest level to achieve their goals. Likewise, collective capacity is manifested in organizations whose members express a shared vision and determination to reach their agreed-upon purpose. In *Leading in a Culture of Change* (2001), Fullan argues that if leaders are to sustain change, they consider building collective capacity as their primary role and responsibility. A leader's effectiveness is then judged by the leadership he creates in others (Fullan, 2001). More recently, Fullan (2010) asserts the power of collective capacity to create "emotional commitment and technical expertise that no amount of individual capacity working alone can come close to matching" (p. xiii). In other words, if an organization is to sustain a change initiative, the leader must foster a collective mind-set in concert with collective capacity to build the momentum for that change—a daunting responsibility for one person to bear.

To support principals as they prepare to enroll teachers in the coaching process, you may want to begin by engaging them in conversations about the change process and how school leaders can effectively facilitate the impending changes that instructional coaching will introduce to their schools. In both formal and informal settings, you might discuss recent successes and challenges principals met with when implementing change. Depending on your principals' experiences in leading change, you may want to facilitate a study using one of the following books and articles on the topic:

Fullan, M. (2008). *The six secrets of change: What the best leaders do to help their organizations survive and thrive.* San Francisco: Jossey-Bass.
Fullan, M. (2010). *Motion leadership: The skinny on becoming change savvy.* Thousand Oaks, CA: Corwin.
Heath, C., & Heath, D. (2011). Overcoming resistance to change. *School Administrator 68*(3), 28–32.
Killion, J. (2008). Courage, confidence, clarity mark the pathway to change. *Journal of Staff Development, 29*(4), 55–59.
Knight, J. (2011). *Unmistakable impact: A partnership approach for dramatically improving instruction.* Thousand Oaks, CA: Corwin.
Senge, P. M. (2006). *The fifth discipline: The art and practice of the learning organization.* New York: Doubleday/Currency.

How Instructional Coaching Supports and Facilitates Change

When introducing instructional coaching to your principals, one of the first things they will want to know is how coaching will support and facilitate the district's (and the individual school's) change initiative. By design, instructional coaches are agents of change. "Coaches have the capacity to question and instill curiosity and doubt, thereby generating dissonance essential to promote change" (Knight, 2009, p. 13). Instructional coaches are able to finesse the change challenge because their role is supportive rather than judgmental. Additionally, as members of the school leadership team, coaches partner with school leaders to develop both individual and collective capacity among teachers. According to Knight (2011), an instructional coach's work "must focus on capacity building if it is to have long-term impact" (p. 98).

You and your leadership team will need to determine the intensity of the professional learning needed to help principals develop a strong understanding of how instructional coaches support and facilitate change. For some people, the connection between coaching and collective capacity building may become quite obvious during initial discussions about the change process. Others may need further study and discussion.

The Role of the Instructional Coach

It is imperative that you spend time with school leaders working to develop an explicit understanding of what an instructional coach is as well as what an instructional coach is not. Enlisting your coaching leadership team and coaching champions (if identified) to facilitate this learning may prove to be an effective and prudent strategy, especially if the team has sufficient time and resources to develop its own clear, in-depth understanding of instructional coaching. If your organization has available funds for hiring an outside expert in the field of coaching to work with principals and other school leaders to develop their understanding of instructional coaching, we strongly encourage you to do so. If funding for leadership professional learning is limited, perhaps you might send a team of administrators to a conference to learn about coaching and to share their learning with the other principals upon their return. Learning Forward's national conference and regional conferences offer a number of sessions on coaching. Jim Knight, whose writings are cited throughout this book, hosts an annual instructional coaching conference near the University of Kansas in Lawrence, Kansas, that is exceptional because it is focused entirely on instructional coaching.

Instructional coaches assume a variety of roles, such as the 10 identified by Killion and Harrison (2006): "resource provider, data coach, instructional specialist, curriculum specialist, classroom supporter, learning facilitator, mentor, school leader, catalyst for change, and learner" (p. 28). As resource providers, coaches are able to assist teachers and principals in locating and/or creating valuable resources related to content, pedagogy, assessment, classroom management, and other pertinent topics. In addition, resource providers keep teachers and school administrators informed of best practices and current research (Killion & Harrison, 2006). As data coaches, instructional coaches work with teachers to interpret formal and informal formative and summative assessment data to improve teaching and learning. In the role of data coach, the coach may also gather data through observations, videotaping, and reflective conferences. The data coach then communicates his or her findings with the teacher as another way of informing teacher practice. Another role that coaches assume is that of instructional specialist. In this role, the coach supports teachers by assisting them in designing differentiated instructional plans based on student needs. The focus for instructional specialists is to support teachers as they implement research-based instructional strategies (Killion & Harrison, 2006).

Closely related to the role of instructional specialist is the role of curriculum specialist. In this role, the instructional coach becomes an expert in curriculum content and standards. As a curriculum specialist, the instructional coach works with teachers to ensure that various initiatives and programs are implemented with fidelity (Killion & Harrison, 2006). While it is unlikely that even the best instructional coaches will be expert in every content area, the expectation for coaches is that they will have enough understanding of the various content standards that they can assist teachers in navigating curriculum guides or facilitate communication between teachers and content specialists in the school or district (Killion & Harrison, 2006).

Instructional coaches are also classroom supporters. Using what Killion and Harrison (2006) refer to as a "gradual release model," instructional coaches employ strategies to support teachers in the early stages of using new instructional strategies or programs until the teacher is ready to use the strategy or program independently and with fidelity. Taking on the role of learning facilitator means the coach provides job-embedded professional development opportunities for teachers. These learning opportunities may include technology integration professional learning, lesson study, standards analysis, and classroom-management strategies, to name a few.

The remaining three roles instructional coaches may assume are mentor, catalyst for change, and learner. Some schools and school systems already have strong mentoring programs in place to assist new teachers; however, instructional coaches should be prepared to work with new teachers, too. As stated earlier, instructional coaches act as change catalysts every time they question the status quo, whether they raise evaluative questions or questions related to continuing long-held practices. They are learners by the very nature of their positions. They must constantly hone their craft by giving time and attention to their own professional learning and growth.

Because of the various roles associated with instructional coaching, it benefits principals to understand what the roles are, to reflect on when and with whom the various coaching roles might apply, and to be able to direct coaches to a specific role if such direction is needed.

> **REFLECT:** Think about the various roles of a coach. Which role do you want your coaches to assume as their primary role? What steps can you take to communicate your preferences to coaches and teachers and to protect time and resources for this particular one?

The Role of the Principal

As previously stated, the role of the principal is key in determining the success of an instructional coaching initiative. Instructional coaching is most successful when the principal and instructional coach work together as partners (Knight, 2005). How the principal decides to introduce the instructional coach to the faculty, what provisions he or she will make for the coach's room or office assignment, and his or her preference for the method and frequency of communication with the coach are some examples of questions the principal must resolve prior to the instructional coach starting to work in the school (Killion, 2007). We found it helpful to generate a list of guiding questions for coaches to ask principals during their initial meeting, scheduled to precede the coach's introduction to the faculty. Coaches asked their principals questions such as, If you went into a classroom, what would you see that would help you predict that the kids will be successful? What district initiatives are most widely implemented in your school? In general, what should the focus of classroom visits and professional conversations between your instructional coach and your teachers be (engaging strategies, use of technology, student and classroom management, etc.)? and How can your instructional coach best assist your school in achieving your school-improvement goals?

From the outset of the principal–coach relationship, the principal should plan and follow through with regularly scheduled meetings with the instructional coach to gather information, provide feedback, ask questions, and address issues that may arise. The principal should also work with the coach and teaching staff to safeguard time set aside for professional learning. An even stronger demonstration of support for coaching occurs each time the principal is able to participate in site-based, job-embedded learning as a colearner. One district leader learned the value of the colearning experience for principals and coaches and reflected her thoughts in a recent article:

> If I could start over, I would have included principals and coaches earlier and more often in shared professional development. The principal's role is too complex and demanding to do it alone. Principals viewed their coach as an ally, and all saw the coach as essential for site-based learning. Coach/principal teams eventually communicated and balanced district initiatives and school-based learning. (Petti, 2010, p. 56)

"As principals and teachers, we must attend not only to our students' learning but also to our own and to that of the adults around us. When we do this, we are on the road to achieving collective responsibility for the school and becoming a community of learners."

—Linda Lambert (2003, p. 3)

The Role of the Coaching Champion

Killion and Harrison (2006) describe a coaching *champion* as someone who advocates for coaches and coaching by giving the day-to-day guidance and support for coaches, and intervening when the coach's role becomes conflicted or when differences arise between the coach and the principal. A coaching champion protects the parameters and the intent of the instructional coaching program while also protecting the roles of the instructional coach. In some instances, the coaching champion takes on the role of mediator, serving to clarify policies and procedures related to the instructional coaching program. Coaching champions are cheerleaders, mentors, coaches of coaches, supervisors, data collectors, schedulers, and advisors whose number one goal is to contribute the necessary support and direction for coaching to succeed as a viable professional development model to strengthen both teaching and learning.

In implementing a large school- or districtwide coaching program, we recommend forming a champion team that can support the champion or champions responsible for individual coaches. If you use this model, along with the champion, the principals must also become familiar with how the champion team will operate. If different champions are responsible for different coaches, principals must be aware of whom they should contact when needs arise.

Communication Among Stakeholders

The lack of effective communication can be the *sticky wicket* in any group or organization, and that is true for an instructional coaching program as well. A fully developed and transparent communication plan should be shared among stakeholders when the instructional coaching program is first rolled out. At the earliest opportunity, principals should delineate their communication expectations with coaches and with all members of their teaching staffs.

According to Barkley (2010), there are four communication models from which to work:

1. a *two-way model* between the principal and teacher and between the coach and teacher, but not between the principal and the coach;

2. a *silent mentor model* in which the principal and teacher talk to each other, the teacher and coach talk to each other, and the principal talks to the coach without expectation of feedback from the instructional coach;

3. the *positive reinforcement model* in which two-way communication exists between the teacher and coach and between the teacher and principal, but only positive information is communicated from the coach to the principal; and

4. a *full communication model* in which the principal, teacher, and instructional coach all communicate with each other, regardless of the positive or negative nature of the communication.

The model of communication that is selected will vary from school to school, district to district. However, as should be expected, a more transparent, open, and honest communication approach tends to breed trust. The more trust, the more people are willing to risk being vulnerable with each other. The more people are willing to risk being vulnerable with each other, the greater the opportunity for growth. To illustrate this point, consider findings from a longitudinal study of appreciative inquiry conducted by M. Tschannen-Moran and Tschannen-Moran (2011): "Trust matters most in situations of interdependence, where people must depend on one another to achieve desired outcomes. This interdependence creates a situation of vulnerability. In such situations, trust is essential to the accomplishment of shared goals" (p. 438). Healthy coaching relationships and capacity building require members of the organization to be vulnerable with themselves and with each other as they become more interdependent. Regardless of the communication model schools or districts choose to use, trust will be one of the most critical components of the collaborative process utilized in coaching.

> *"In coaching, the conversation between the coach and the coachee forms the key to the relationship. Communication creates the trust . . . It uncovers the coachee's agenda, vision, and beliefs. It helps explore options and strategies, tactics, and the focus of the teaching, along with the personal and professional development of the individual."*
>
> —Stephen Barkley (2010, p. 52)

REFLECT: Which of Barkley's (2010) four communication models appeals to your communication style and the needs of your organization?

The Principal–Coach Memorandum of Understanding

A memorandum of understanding (MOU) is simply a written agreement between two parties that outlines each party's commitments to the other in their working relationship. When the principal and coach begin their work together to form a leadership partnership, it is helpful to record in an MOU those agreed-upon expectations, commitments, and assignments so that time, hectic schedules, and urgent yet important additions to everyone's agendas do not steer the instructional coach and/or his work with the school away from school and district goals. The MOU does not have to be complicated or fixed. Similar to an action plan, it should be revisited periodically and jointly by the principal and instructional coach to track progress and make adjustments as needed. The MOU can simply reflect the school's vision or mission statement, the primary goals the principal wants the instructional coach to address, the primary coaching approaches agreed upon by the principal and coach, and the method and frequency of communication between the coach and principal (as well as the communication model that will be used in the school). In our district, we also asked coaches to identify at least one coaching goal per school each year. See Chapter 5 resources for a sample principal–coach MOU.

> **REFLECT:** What coaching expectations, commitments, and assignments do you want to discuss with your coach? What expectations and commitments can the coach count on from you?

Voices From the Field

We have found that principals especially enjoy learning from each other. Sometimes they take the initiative and start their own peer coaching activities among themselves to gain greater insight into leading their schools toward greater collaboration. The following are some pieces of advice principals wished to pass along:

High School Principal Dr. Ron Becker suggests encouraging each teacher to reflect on one area in which he or she can use the coach.

"Sell the program, but keep it voluntary and collaborative and student focused. It would be a mistake to require a certain level of involvement and then create resentment."

Middle School Principal Andrew Turner agrees: "The principal should become as knowledgeable as possible about the roles and responsibilities of an instructional coach. One must be able to effectively communicate this initiative to the entire staff. The principal and coach must have the same focus for the school and be able to outline the steps and procedures to attain measurable success."

Elementary School Principal Danny Sullivan believes it is best to pick a teacher leader from each grade level and ask the coach to work with that person first. He says, "Talk to the teachers about the benefits of coaching and train the teachers and staff to see the big picture—this could totally change the overall school environment and look of the classroom in a very positive way!"

Instructional Coach Karen Marklein felt her principal was key to her effectiveness. She would advise others to follow suit and push their teachers to grow. "Principals have to believe in the coaching program," Marklein said. "Teachers naturally follow their leadership, and if the principal does not support the coach, the principal cannot expect improvement in student achievement. In my experience, a coaching program does not just happen. A successful coaching program is the result of a symbiotic relationship between the principal and the coach, and among the coach and the faculty. When it works, it is a beautiful thing."

A Sample Plan for Preparing Principals for Coaching

- Rollout of districtwide instructional coaching program details to all principals and supervisors.
- All principals and supervisors read one book that aligns with the organization's vision for coaching.
- All principals and supervisors participate in K–12 meetings to develop a shared understanding of what an instructional coach is and what an instructional coach is not.
- All principals and supervisors participate in formal professional learning event with a coaching expert or someone who has extensive firsthand knowledge of coaching.

- All principals and instructional coaches participate in celebratory breakfast that includes shared learning opportunities.
- Coaching champions schedule onsite interviews between coaches and their assigned principals. A coaching champion escorts each coach to the interviews to act as timekeeper and to redirect questions should the conversation stray from the predetermined guided questions.
- Periodic onsite and/or telephone interviews between coaching champions and principals.
- Periodic discussion of coaching questions and concerns in regularly scheduled grade-level and K–12 principal meetings.

Including the coaching champion in the initial on-site principal–coach interviews is especially helpful when using a district model for your coaching program, as many of your coaches and principals may have no prior shared working experience. The coaching champion's presence also demonstrates district-level support for the principal, the coach, and the coaching program.

REFLECT: Jot down a list of first steps you want to take in preparing principals to launch an instructional coaching initiative in your district. Who needs to be part of the principal-preparation planning process? What is your time frame within which you must work?

Summary

1. The principal is key to the success of an instructional coaching program.

2. Preparing principals to implement an instructional coaching program should include topics such as leading for change, how coaching supports and facilitates change, the role of the instructional coach, the role of the principal, the role of the coaching champion, communication among stakeholders, and the principal–coach MOU.

3. A sample principal-preparation plan may include required reading, small- and large-group principal meetings, consulting an outside expert, initial principal–coach interviews facilitated by the coaching champion, and opportunities for periodic progress monitoring.

"People don't at first follow worthy causes. They follow worthy leaders who promote worthwhile causes" (Maxwell, 2001, p. 155). A well-constructed principal-preparation plan will enable worthy principal leaders to successfully implement your district's instructional coaching initiative.

Building an Instructional Coaching Program for Maximum Capacity

1. Research coaching and coaching models. Reach out to others (coaches, coaching champions) in the professional community. (Chapter 1)

2. Select a "champion team" who will develop the coaching initiative and will support coaching. (Chapter 2)

3. Develop a shared vision of instructional coaching for your school or district. (Chapter 2)

4. Align your vision of instructional coaching with your school or district's vision. (Chapter 2)

5. Develop an administrative model for coaching. (Chapter 2)

6. Develop your assessment plan for the coaching initiative. Know what you will evaluate and how you will do it. (Chapter 3)

7. Know the five characteristics of great coaches prior to hiring and assigning, and use them to develop a recruitment strategy. Interview and hire coaches. (Chapter 4)

8. Determine preservice training needs for administrators and supervisors and develop a learning plan. (Chapter 5)

9. **Determine preservice training needs for newly hired instructional coaches and develop a learning plan for the first of the school year as part of a long-term comprehensive model of ongoing professional learning and support. (Chapter 6)**

10. Plan for opportunities for regular collaboration among and between coaches and teachers after coaches begin. (Chapter 7)

11. Develop a model of ongoing learning and support for instructional coaches. (Chapter 8)

12. Evaluate your coaching program and make necessary adjustments to sustain, change, abandon, or reimagine your coaching initiative. (Chapters 3 and 9)

6

Anchors Aweigh

Preparing Coaches
Through Preservice Instruction

> *"We must sail, sometimes with the wind, and sometimes against it. But we must not drift or lie at anchor."*
>
> —Oliver Wendell Holmes (2001)

A shared vision and goals determine your organization's destination while also enabling you to determine the essential knowledge and skills your coaches need to be fully equipped to support those goals. As you plan how you wish to prepare your coaches to begin their first year of coaching, review your organization's vision and goals as well as the goals you set for the coaching program and use them as a basis for the first phase of a comprehensive ongoing learning plan for your coaches. The preservice planning team should devote significant time to aligning the vision and goals of the coaching program with those of the organization. Time spent in this alignment process will result in a more sharply focused understanding of the *big picture* of your coaching program and will help new coaches understand how their work supports the big picture of your school or district's vision and goals.

> Preservice instruction is only the initial point of learning for your instructional coaches. Just like teachers and administrators, coaches also need the ongoing, sustained support of job-embedded professional learning throughout the year as described in Chapter 8.

Prioritize Specific Knowledge and Skill Sets to Deepen and Refine

In Chapter 4, we outlined six imperative qualities of coaches based on our experience and research. While the coaches you hire must be visionary, courageous, masterful teachers, balanced, treasured, and embody arête (excellence), we admit that all of the qualities are manifested in varying degrees in any new coach. Additionally, the coaches' understanding of your school or district's strengths, challenges, and improvement goals may be limited, especially if newly hired coaches are also new to your district. In many cases, their knowledge of coaching theory and practical coaching skills may be rudimentary. It will be up to you and your planning team to prioritize the specific knowledge and skill sets you want coaches to deepen and refine during preservice instruction.

To assist you as you begin this process, imagine what a highly effective coach looks and sounds like as he or she works with teachers and principals to improve student achievement in *your* school or district. Certainly, if he or she is a masterful teacher, the highly effective coach will have exceptional content knowledge and pedagogical skills. In general, preservice programs will not need to address these types of skills, as they are prerequisites for hiring. Your vision of a highly effective coach, however, may include particular skill sets that your new coaches may not have fully developed. For example, while they may be visionary, beginning coaches may need help in expanding their vision beyond the four classroom walls to be able to understand the district's *big picture*. New coaches may need to deepen their understanding of recently implemented school or district initiatives such as assessment models, technology plans, special education programs, or new curriculum standards.

In addition, beginning coaches, regardless of their level of communication skills, may need specific instruction in conflict management to assist them in responding to any "pushback" they might encounter in their new roles. Likewise, no matter how strong their background in coaching might be, new coaches will benefit from further instruction on the praxis of instructional coaching. This might include structured observations, coaching conversations, protocols, coaching moves, and coaching strategies.

Finally, your coaches must begin to form a team—with each other, with the coaching champion, and with principals and other administrative staff with whom they will work. As Saphier and West (2009) explain,

> In order to have the wherewithal to assist teachers and principals to improve instruction and learning, coaches need a great deal of expertise in a wide variety of things: content knowledge, pedagogical knowledge, change theory, interpersonal skills, big-picture/long-term visioning and planning, etc. An individual is unlikely to have such a complete skill set at the onset of a coaching initiative; therefore the district will want to set up systems so coaches can learn from their coaching colleagues, the leadership team, and outside consultants. (p. 50)

REFLECT: What specific knowledge and skill sets will your coaches need in order to best support your organization's vision and goals? How would you prioritize these?

Develop a Preservice Instruction Plan

It is often said that to have a great ending, you have to have a great beginning. A well-developed preservice instruction plan will include the essential knowledge and skills to equip your coaches and your coaching program for a great beginning and, consequently, for the great ending that you want to achieve. The preservice plan will require you to identify the experts in your organization (and perhaps outside, as well) who will be responsible for leading professional learning activities during the preservice instruction period. The plan will also address issues such as time and timing, location, and resources.

> The ultimate great ending for an instructional coaching program is a school or district's total immersion in a culture of collaboration and collegiality, where individual and collective capacity are maximized and valued by stakeholders at all levels of the organization—where everyone, including administrators, gives and receives coaching support!

Champion the Vision

New instructional coaches will have the responsibility of championing the district's vision as well as the belief systems that drive the district's vision. Coaches will also need to understand the vision and belief systems of the individual schools they serve. However, it is insufficient to simply know and understand the vision and belief systems. If student achievement and learning are to improve, the vision and beliefs must be put into action—at the individual teacher level, grade group or department level, and school level. Preservice instruction for instructional coaches is incomplete without intentional, thorough discussion of the mission and vision of the school or district and explicit direction about how coaches can carry this out. Expectations for the coaches' role in sharing the mission and vision should be communicated explicitly during preservice professional learning, and coaches should practice articulating that mission and vision themselves.

Speak the Language

Coaches should spend some preservice learning time examining vocabulary and language specific to your organization's initiatives to clarify any misunderstanding or misuse of terminology. Coaches must use the correct terminology to communicate the school or district's mission, vision, and beliefs, and it should be in the kind of language used by the rest of the school or district. I did not realize how important this was until I was in a school district talking with teachers about pursuing a graduate program at a university where I worked. Other admissions people had come to answer their questions about the program, but until someone who "spoke the language" of local public education talked with them, they were hesitant that the program would meet their needs. I think this was true for two reasons: first, because academic terminology seemed to differ from the practical information they needed for their jobs at the time, even though it was likely essentially the same thing; second, the common language gave them a sense of comfort and collegiality. We were on the same team—we knew and valued the same things.

> *"If you want to build a ship, don't herd people together to collect wood and don't assign them tasks and work, but rather teach them to long for the endless immensity of the sea."*
>
> —often attributed to
> Antoine de Saint-Exupery (n.d.)

Know the Community You Serve

As new *coaching champions*, we wanted to follow Saint-Exupery's advice as we endeavored to instill a vision of coaching into our newly hired coaches. We felt that before they could "long for the immensity of the sea," they needed to experience the immensity of our school district. How better to do that than to get on a bus and see it all! So we planned a bus tour of the entire school district as one of the initial preservice learning activities. The new instructional coaching staff and coach facilitators loaded onto a school bus to begin a cross-county tour of nearly 50 elementary, middle, and high schools. Eight of the coaches were designated *community guides* to provide a brief overview of each community served by their local schools. The overview included demographic information, history, and fun or interesting facts about the community—each not more than a 5-minute snapshot. All the coaches knew their school assignments by that time, and they perked up with excitement when we drove past *their* schools. The purpose of the field trip experience was to demonstrate the diversity of the district to instructional coaches who had never been in the community in which they were now going to serve. The trip was long (close to 200 miles!!) and the bus was not the most comfortable mode of transportation, but it provided an early opportunity for the new coaches to begin to grasp the district's big picture—the "immensity of the sea."

Embrace the Role of Change Facilitator

When we arrived back at our starting point after a long, hot school bus ride (think: August in the South!) the coaches were greeted with an ice cream sundae bar ... chocolate, vanilla, and strawberry ice cream with every topping imaginable from whipped cream to M&Ms to Oreo Cookie crumbles! Those ice cream sundaes were not just good—they were fabulous! The point? **Coaches must embrace their roles as facilitators of change rather than guardians of mediocrity**. Who wants a mediocre ice cream sundae? And who wants a mediocre school or district? Like the long bus ride, coaching acts that facilitate change can create a sense of professional discomfort for teachers, causing them to question their current practices, (Barkley, 2010). Reflective questioning, guided by the instructional coach, opens the door to change. Once the door is open, the coach can encourage and support the teacher's walk through the change threshold. According to Reeves (2009), effective coaching can foster successful change by affecting both individual and small-group behaviors. If instructional coaches are to be the catalysts for change schools and districts intend for them to be, then sufficient preservice learning time should be devoted to key topics such as building trust, collaborating, and understanding the adult learner.

> **REFLECT:** What are some "big picture" concepts you want your coaches to grasp before they begin their coaching journey? What kind of memorable activity could you provide your new coaches to help them grasp the *immensity of the sea* as it relates to your organization?

Understand Coaching Roles

After grasping the immensity of the sea and the dangers of mediocrity, all new coaches feel the need for professional learning that addresses the practice of coaching, including the various roles that coaches assume as they work with teachers and administrators. The art and science of coaching takes time to develop. You may want to consider designating at least 3 days of preservice learning for explicit instruction in the roles of coaching such as Killian and Harrison (2006) identify and describe. At any given time, a coach is a resource provider, data coach, curriculum specialist, instructional specialist, classroom supporter, mentor, learning facilitator, school leader, catalyst for change, and learner. Just as teachers change hats throughout the school day to meet the needs of their students, coaches will change hats to meet the needs of their schools and teachers.

Once your coaches become familiar with the various coaching roles, you may want to provide a general indication of how much time they should allocate to each role. Time spent in any given role will vary with the unique needs and goals of each school. For example, one school may launch a new schoolwide technology initiative, and the principal may want the instructional coach to spend the majority of her time working with teachers to integrate technology into the curriculum—requiring the coach to be curriculum specialist, instructional specialist, learning facilitator, catalyst for change, and leader. Another school may have a large number of new teachers, in which case the coach may spend a high percentage of his time facilitating a new teacher PLC—here, the coach spends much of his time working as a learning facilitator, resource provider, and classroom supporter.

Understand *Holonomy*

Important to remember as you plan your preservice instruction is a concept that I first learned more than a decade ago as a participant in an in-depth cognitive coaching course developed for school leaders in my state. The concept is *holonomy*, "the state of being simultaneously a part and a whole" (Costa & Garmston, 2002)—a dichotomy that exists for all teachers. Teachers are a part of a larger system, namely the school and the school district. At the same time, they are autonomous in their ability to make their own teaching decisions, motivate themselves to action, and monitor and regulate their own personal and professional behaviors. The same is true of instructional coaches. As you plan your preservice activities, consider opportunities for coaches to learn with and from district-level supervisors, coordinators, and directors. By including such opportunities, you will address what we like to call *horizontal* and *vertical* holonomy. The individual coach (part) and her role in the coaching program (whole) represent horizontal holonomy. The individual coach (part) and her role in the school or district (whole) represent vertical holonomy. Coaches must have a clear understanding of their responsibilities to themselves, the coaching program, and their schools and school districts.

REFLECT: Think about the first day your coaches will enter their schools. How far in advance of their start date will you be able to start your preservice instruction? How much time will you need to allot for preservice learning in order to accomplish your preservice learning goals?

Don't Forget the Captain!

Preservice activities for new coaches should include time for coaches to meet with their principals prior to starting their coaching positions in schools. Initial meetings between coach and principal must be intentional, purposeful, and facilitated—before the coach ever steps foot in the school.

As we planned our preservice learning, we decided to arrange two meetings between the coaches and their principals. The first meeting would be a celebration—a "Breakfast of Champions"—where all coaches and principals joined with district-level staff members to officially launch the coaching program. The first part of the breakfast celebration focused on building relationships between the coaches and their principals. Once the meal was finished, we distributed an article recommended to us by coaching consultant Steve Barkley titled "Seventeen Reasons Why Football is Better Than High School" (Childress, 1998). In this article, Childress contrasts the highly motivational experience of being on a football team with the experience of being a typical student in a typical high school. Coaches and principals participated in a jigsaw activity using the article as a basis for professional dialog about quality teaching, learning, and student motivation. Our Breakfast of Champions accomplished several important purposes: (1) It served as an icebreaker for coaches and principals meeting for the first time; (2) it set a tone of success for the new coaching program, the coaches, the principals, and their schools; and (3) it generated an air of shared excitement and anticipation for unknown possibilities.

For our second meeting, we arranged for coaches to interview each of their principals using a prepared list of guiding questions. The coaches and principals were given the questions well in advance for reflection, and the coaches were given opportunities to practice asking the questions and responding to potential principal questions and concerns. As coaching champions, we met our coaches at their various school sites and served as facilitators of the meetings, offering input only when the conversation stalled or veered off topic.

Principal/Coach Questions:

Acknowledging the role of the principal as key to the success of any instructional coaching program, we invite you to participate in the orientation process for new coaches by being available to meet with your coach facilitator and instructional coach in a brief meeting structured around the following questions:

1. When you visit classrooms, what student and teacher behaviors do you look for to indicate that students are learning?

2. What district initiatives are most successfully implemented in your school?

3. In general, what should the focus of classroom visits and professional conversations between your instructional coach and your teachers be?

4. How can your instructional coach best assist your school in achieving your school-improvement goals?

You may think it unnecessary for coaches to practice before interviewing the principal or for the coaching champion to be present during the interviews—the coaches are professionals, aren't they? However, believing that great beginnings lead to great endings, we wanted our new coaches to have the utmost confidence in themselves and to have no doubt as to the support they could count on from their coaching champions.

Summary

The title of this chapter, "Anchors Aweigh," is a metaphor for freeing new instructional coaches to embark on their voyage, supporting the organization in its vision and goals. The anchor is hoisted through an intentional, intensive preservice instruction plan for new coaches. To develop and implement an effective preservice instruction plan, the leadership team should consider the following:

1. What are the specific knowledge and skill sets we want our coaches to deepen and refine?

2. Who are the experts in our organization who will be responsible for leading professional learning activities during the preservice period?

3. What district and/or school goals or initiatives do we want to address during preservice learning?

4. How much time should we allot for implementing our preservice learning plan?

5. How far in advance of the coaches' first day in their schools can we start preservice professional learning?

6. What resources are available to us to implement our plan effectively?

A well-planned, comprehensive preservice professional learning program will direct the crew toward the school or district's destination and provide the impetus to hoist anchor, freeing beginning coaches to assume new leadership roles in their schools or districts. Equipped with the essential knowledge and skills needed to fulfill their coaching responsibilities and motivated by the immensity of the sea, new coaches can move forward with greater confidence in their abilities and greater understanding of their purpose. Anchors aweigh!

Building an Instructional Coaching Program for Maximum Capacity

1. Research coaching and coaching models. Reach out to others (coaches, coaching champions) in the professional community. (Chapter 1)

2. Select a "champion team" who will develop the coaching initiative and will support coaching. (Chapter 2)

3. Develop a shared vision of instructional coaching for your school or district. (Chapter 2)

4. Align your vision of instructional coaching with your school or district's vision. (Chapter 2)

5. Develop an administrative model for coaching. (Chapter 2)

6. Develop your assessment plan for the coaching initiative. Know what you will evaluate and how you will do it. (Chapter 3)

7. Know the five characteristics of great coaches prior to hiring and assigning, and use them to develop a recruitment strategy. Interview and hire coaches. (Chapter 4)

8. Determine preservice training needs for administrators and supervisors and develop a learning plan. (Chapter 5)

9. Determine preservice training needs for newly hired instructional coaches and develop a learning plan for the first of the school year as part of a long-term comprehensive model of ongoing professional learning and support. (Chapter 6)

10. Plan for opportunities for regular collaboration among and between coaches and teachers after coaches begin. (Chapter 7)

11. Develop a model of ongoing learning and support for instructional coaches. (Chapter 8)

12. Evaluate your coaching program and make necessary adjustments to sustain, change, abandon, or reimagine your coaching initiative. (Chapters 3 and 9)

7

All Hands on Deck

Preparing the Teachers and Staff

As we were developing our coaching program, we joked about building the airplane while we were flying it. But that was not entirely accurate. I have seen an airplane land on an aircraft carrier with unbelievable speed and precision. I have never seen anyone change a school that way. The image that really resonated with us was that of a large ship approaching the dock. It goes very slowly, and sometimes it seems like it is heading the wrong way, but finally, after much slow and steady progress, it reaches the dock. But even then the goal is not achieved . . . someone with a rope has to tie on and pull it in. When building a coaching program, you have to have a boatswain who knows the ropes and can call all hands to pull the coach and school together.

Smooth Sailing or Rough Seas?

Although we are talking about a coaching *program*, coaching is actually just one piece of an overall culture of collaboration and embedded professional learning. Coaches are simply an excellent way to leverage the strengths already inherent in an organization or individual to bring them to their maximum capacity. To be most effective, each coach would be placed in a school where a significant number of teachers are professionals who desire to improve and where the principal is an instructional leader. They would start their first day of coaching in a school where the interactions among the faculty, staff and administration are functional and mature, and perhaps where some movement has already been made toward a collaborative culture. We have been privileged to work in and with schools in which this is the case, and there, coaching has flourished.

Unfortunately, this is not always the case. In some schools or districts, coaches are placed in a school with a dispirited leader and a faculty looking for transfers. Test scores are low, students are unmotivated, parents are uninvolved, and the morale is abysmal. The needs in this case are beyond the scope of one or two coaches, no matter how prepared and hardworking. Coaching can make an impact in such a place and should be a part of a comprehensive improvement plan, but absolute turnaround requires more than what can reasonably be expected from a coach alone without strong administrative support. For this reason, it is our view that when resources are limited, coaches should be assigned to schools that already have the leadership in place to use them effectively. This is a simple principle I discovered in the 1990s when studying implementation of instructional technology in schools—the schools that used technology to improve instruction were those in which the leadership, faculty, and staff were trained and ready for it. If they were not ready, the dusty boxes of computers stood unopened in storage closets under stacks of student projects and lost overcoats. My conclusions then are our conclusions now. If you can, take the time to prepare the cultural groundwork for any major change.

If you and your team have had the luxury of a long implementation period, by the time coaching starts, you would have had time to involve all of your staff and faculty in the planning process. To be realistic, this is seldom the case in education. For that reason, you may want to look at preparing your staff from two different perspectives: the first, for those of you who have the luxury of time and, the second, for those of you who, like us, were forced by circumstance to plan and implement a coaching program virtually overnight.

Start With the Best

In *Things Fall Apart*, Achebe's (1992) classic novel about the impact of colonialism on Africa, a white missionary encounters the Igbu tribe. The leaders of the tribe resist the missionary's advances in an attempt to preserve their status, culture, and way of life. A group of outcasts, however, who have long been mistreated by the tribe's leaders, are attracted to the foreigner's message. The missionary targets this group for conversion, and it cements in the minds of the tribe that Christianity is for the weak. This story has gone through my mind when I have seen coaches focus their work with the teachers who are marginalized in a school culture and ignore those who are influential and respected by the majority of the staff. From the very beginning, it is important that administrators and coaches recognize that to change a culture, the individuals with the most influence in the culture must be convinced first, and others will follow. You must anticipate the potential reactions of groups or individuals in your school who may feel marginalized or superseded by the coaching program. This might include mentors, reading specialists, or other professionals who act as coaches in some way. You cannot have a group of powerful and respected resisters in your school and expect the other teachers to support coaching. The coaching champions must reach out to this group first, so that their valuable insight and support are gained.

Administrators must also reach out to teacher leaders and elicit their support, emphasizing that coaches are there to work with everyone in the building, but most especially those that are already good teachers. Of course, in a perfect world, the most hardworking, dedicated, knowledgeable, and passionate teachers in the building should have been involved from the beginning in the coaching planning process. This is ideally accomplished through the effective implementation of professional learning communities and peer coaching. Over time, as teachers begin to work more deeply with each other, they see the benefits of collaboration. Expanding this experience with a full-time coach seems natural when learning teams have been effective. This bottom-up approach to coaching implementation combined with top-down support from the administration and district sets the stage for a successful program. Unfortunately, especially when a coaching program is rushed in the planning phase, building support among teacher leaders can get left out. In one school, individuals who worked in the new teacher mentor program felt that their turf was being invaded by the coaching program, and until roles were articulated, there was conflict. This misunderstanding could have been avoided if the coaching champions had taken steps to explain the differences in the two programs and how they would work hand in hand.

> **REFLECT:** Consider your school or district. What entrenched programs or job positions might feel marginalized by a new coaching program? What steps can you take to avoid this?

If teachers have not been involved in professional learning communities yet, a visioning process in which the staff looks at the school vision and identifies ways to move toward that vision can be a good first step. From this point, the administrator or coaching champion can facilitate research and book studies on collaborative learning either with the whole staff or with a smaller group of mini-champions.

Develop Mini-Champions

Gladwell, in the bestseller *The Tipping Point* (2002), argues that a few people in an organization can make an idea catch on. He calls this principle the Law of the Few. Three types of people, whom he terms *mavens, connectors*, and *salesmen*, can make the difference in whether an idea spreads. Although people are more complex than these labels, it does seem to be a remarkably convenient way of looking at the kinds of teacher leaders who can influence the acceptance of a new idea like coaching in a school setting. A *maven* is a collector of knowledge. This teacher makes a hobby of trying the latest instructional technology strategy and can name the latest books by education gurus. These are the people in a work setting that tempt the rest of us to skip an inservice session or enjoy a crime novel instead of that new book on classroom management. They went, they read the book, they read every article about the topic, and they can tell you which articles you should or should not read. They may even copy the article, highlight the pertinent passages, and put it in your faculty mailbox. Mavens want research and data, and they can see through things that are the not grounded in sound research and best practices. These are the folks who actually want to read all the research about coaching. If you have a maven or two in the building, set them on the task of research before the coaching program is implemented. Not only will they give you the information you need, they will also spread the word to their colleagues who like to borrow their notes.

Connectors are people who have wide circles of acquaintances and are not limited to small cliques (Gladwell, 2002). They are on friendly terms with almost everyone in a school—even a large school—and usually know many people at other nearby schools and in the community as well. They like to introduce people to each other and figure out who is related to whom. They may not rush out to either hurt or help the program, but they may have casual conversations with large numbers of people in the community. These people must have a good understanding of coaching so their vast communication network gets the right information. They can be the key to spreading the word about the effectiveness of coaching. Coaches themselves are often connectors, and this makes it easier for them to network with teachers.

Although Gladwell (2002) uses the term *salesmen* for the final group, the term *persuader* works better in the school setting. If you take a salesman out of the showroom and put him in the classroom, he might be that teacher that just sparkles with emotional energy and empathy. These are not people who try to sell you something you don't want; instead, they discern others' emotions and can draw them into their own emotions. They are masters of connecting with people and making them feel the same way they do about things. Many great teachers are persuaders. They are the ones who actually get the kids to love Shakespeare or the Pythagorean Theorem. They can also get their colleagues excited about things. Reaching these people is job one in an instructional coaching program in a school or district. If they are on board, others will follow.

Every program needs a champion, but it also needs lots of minichampions in a building. A good administrator will discuss coaching with many small groups of teachers, get input and diffuse concerns, and find a few mavens, connectors, and persuaders to become mini-champions. These people should be persuaded to be among the first to step up and participate in coaching. If they understand what coaching is and connect coaching with their identity as excellent teachers, others will follow. People do what they see others do.

> **REFLECT:** Consider the personalities in a school with which you work. Can you identify mavens, connectors, and persuaders? Do you think Gladwell's categories are accurate and beneficial? Why or why not?

Connect Coaching to One's School and Personal Vision

Teachers are information workers—they think for a living. As we mentioned early on, these professionals who do complex work are motivated by mastery, autonomy, and purpose (Pink, 2009). As a college student, I waited tables at a local restaurant part time. I must admit, I hated the job . . . except when I was asked to train the new wait staff. It thrilled me to be able to show them how to do part of the job and then watch them do it successfully. In school, I had that same wonderful feeling when I did an assignment and knew it was really good—to tell the truth, these experiences are among the reasons I became a teacher. That feeling of mastery can be challenged by the idea of coaching. Teachers may fear that when a coach or colleague comes to watch them do what they think they do well, they will be faced with the possibility that they have not mastered their craft after all! Coaching brings discomfort, and that, in turn, brings growth. But the discomfort is, well, uncomfortable. . . . But according to Vanderburg and Stephens (2009), teachers found that working with a coach provided a "renewed sense of themselves as professionals who took risks and who grounded their instructional decision both in their knowledge of their students and in the knowledge of research and theory" (p. 2). Teachers can learn to see that coaching, in addition to bringing discomfort, leads to a sense of mastery.

Another hurdle is that teachers are motivated by choice and freedom. When something feels mandated, it will meet with resistance. How then to provide opportunities for mastery, choice, and autonomy while making it clear that collegiality is expected? Coaching must be grounded in the idea of choice but connected to the vision and purpose that the school has already agreed upon. Teachers, like all thinking professionals, are motivated by a sense of purpose. For most, that sense of purpose is what led them to a career in education. Helping teachers see that the purpose of coaching is to support the vision of the school and their vision of themselves as professionals can go a long way in paving the way for the day the coaching program begins. Coaches in one study found that in their experience "change . . . was not a mirror of externally imposed mandates, but instead, change was synonymous with agency" (Vanderburg & Stephens, 2009, p. 2).

Accept Resistance

Change inevitably encounters resistance. As anyone who has tried to change a habit knows, changing your own mind is difficult, and changing others' minds is even more so! Adults struggle from cognitive laxity—it is easier not to change your mind! This is even more apparent when the idea or practice that must be changed comes out of an emotional commitment, such as a teacher's view of what it means to be a professional. Gardner (2006) stated that "The more emotional one's commitment to a cause or belief, the more difficult to change" (p. 57). Gardner goes on to identify the tension that comes between cognitive laxity and the desire for new knowledge. This tension, again, is uncomfortable, both within our own minds and within an organization. It is not, however, a time to back away from the issue. Sometimes these moments of confusion and frustration are just what we need to lead us to new understandings.

Hone the Message

Although coaching has been around in schools for a very long time, it has been our experience that there is a lot of misunderstanding about the role of coaches and the purpose of coaching. Districts and schools envision coaching in many different ways, and sometimes these ways stray far from a collaborative partnership model. Some faculties have no knowledge of coaching at all other than athletic coaching. One teacher told us that before coaching, she had a vision of a coach as her high school PE teacher who laughed at her for missing free throws on the basketball court and yelled at her when she didn't dress out. The job of the school-based administrator or coaching champion is to uncover these erroneous impressions of coaching and replace them with others that are, as D. Heath and Heath (2007) would say, equally "sticky."

Use Sticky Ideas

Heath and Heath (2007) defined sticky ideas as ones that are simple, unexpected, concrete, credible, emotional, and can be related through stories. The very idea of coaching is a simple one—almost so simple it is hard to explain! Barkley (2010) explains it this way: "The farther up the ladder of success one goes, the more coaching is needed. It's what I call the Tiger Woods syndrome" (p. 18). After learning about the Tiger Woods syndrome, one coach in our district, to explain her role and purpose with one compelling image, placed a life-size cutout of Tiger Woods outside her office with the sign, "How many coaches does Tiger have?" The concept—that in sports, the better you are, the more coaches you have—is a sticky one, and she expressed it in a sticky way: a simple question with a simple, believable answer (lots!), an unexpected and concrete visual (Tiger Woods in the hall of a school), and the emotion of something amusing. We used a similar concept by developing a Breakfast of Champions theme with a cereal box to remind teachers to "start their day right" with coaching.

As we all know from advertising, something can be catchy, but we don't trust it . . . as I surf the Internet, I am bombarded by sticky ads: "The amazing cure to wrinkles that has dermatologists around the world angry!" "The one miracle food that will cause you to lose 50 pounds in one month without dieting!" Yes, they get my attention, but I know better than to even click on them . . . they are not credible. Being credible in coaching means two things: First, you are honest and transparent about all aspects of the coaching process and program, and second, you model the model of coaching.

In a recent interview of a faculty member, we asked what the differences were in the different principals she had worked for, what made the difference in a good principal and an average principal. She immediately said, "The good principal didn't ask us to do anything he wasn't willing to do himself." The same holds true in coaching. Many coaching programs for principals and even district superintendents exist, and the principal who participates in this has the added benefit of being a role model for her staff. Coaches often coach each other in their own coaching interactions. The principal may also ask her school's coach to coach her from the very beginning—observing and giving feedback on meetings and professional learning that the principal may lead. This willingness to be vulnerable on the part of the leader and coach will fortify others to take part in the coaching process. It will also help the leader understand the feelings of the staff.

Tell a Story, Be a Part of a Story

> *"Stories are the most effective ways of changing minds . . . there has to be a protagonist. There has to be a goal. There have to be obstacles people can identify with. There has to be an ultimate resolution—hopefully a positive one . . . what leaders do is put aside or reject the old story, the story you have grown up with. Leaders say, 'No it's a different story. You may not like it initially, but it's a better story in the long run, and you have to go with it and here is why . . .'"*
>
> —Howard Gardner (2006)

We hold on vigorously to our most tightly held emotional beliefs, but our beliefs can change or evolve based both on stories we are told and the story that we feel we are living out as we strive toward our vision and purpose in life. Drama is full of moments when an individual begins to see himself as a part of a larger story . . . it is played out in religion, in teams, in corporations, in schools. Why are we drawn to movies or plays in which the underdog suddenly sees himself as part of something bigger and knows he can do something meaningful? We want to have this sense of a greater purpose ourselves. One of the finest examples of this in literature is King Henry's speech in Act 4, scene 2 of Shakespeare's play *Henry V*. The setting is the Hundred Years' War on the eve of the battle of

Agincourt, St. Crispin's Day. England is outnumbered by France and the troops want to desert. Henry tells a story of the future, a vision, of what it will be like when the battle is over. He takes the soldiers' minds away from the fears and struggles of the present and focuses them on the moment when they can stand up proudly, show their wounds to their neighbors, tell the story of the battle, and tell their children of their heroic deeds. This is a vision of a man, a part of a "band of brothers" who will always be proud that they made the right choice:

> *This story shall the good man teach his son;*
>
> *And Crispin Crispian shall ne'er go by,*
>
> *From this day to the ending of the world,*
>
> *But we in it shall be remember'd;*
>
> *We few, we happy few, we band of brothers;*
>
> *For he to-day that sheds his blood with me*
>
> *Shall be my brother; be he ne'er so vile,*
>
> *This day shall gentle his condition: And gentlemen in England now a-bed*
>
> *Shall think themselves accursed they were not here,*
>
> *And hold their manhoods cheap whiles any speaks*
>
> *That fought with us upon Saint Crispin's day. (Henry V, Act 1, scene 2)*

While none of us is Shakespeare, we can use stories both of what has happened in the past and what will happen in the future to help each other remember that our cause here is as great as the English army on the field of Agincourt—we are fighting for the future of our students—and whatever discomfort may come in the short term will be far outweighed by the pride we will have in our accomplishment and the relationships we will forge with each other. A story can answer the two questions that we all have when we are confronted with a challenge: Will it be worth the risk? Will I be able to do it? (Patterson, Grenny, Maxfield, McMillan, & Switzler, 2008).

Know Your Goal: A Culture of Collegiality

Coaching must be set in a healthy cultural context. Throwing a coach overboard in a sea of sharks is a recipe for disaster. One lone coach can make little difference in a highly toxic environment. One district has had a coaching program that has been less effective than it could have been. The reason: Coaches were assigned to schools that were on life support and had only a few months left to survive. In one case, a school had already been informed that it would be reconstituted the next year; this hardly gave the team a reason to want a coach. In that context, neither could be effective. Remember that your goal is not to have a coaching *program*; it is to have a healthy professional culture in which the capacity of teachers, leaders, and students is maximized.

> *"The nature of relationships among the adults within a school has a greater influence on the character and quality of that school and on student accomplishment than anything else."*
>
> —Roland Barth (2006, p. 8)

Gladwell (2002) points out that to bring about fundamental change in people's beliefs and behavior, you must create a community in which those beliefs are "practiced and expressed and nurtured" (p. 173). We spend a lot of time looking at the relationships between student and teacher but relatively little examining relationships between teachers themselves. We may have this backward. According to Barth (2006), the four types of relationships you find in schools are: parallel play, in which teachers work side by side as if the other does not exist; adversarial, in which open war has been waged among teachers; congenial, in which social interaction is pleasant; and collegial, in which conversations revolve around practice, craft, and student achievement, and teachers root for each other's success. Faculties will know if they are in an adversarial relationship, but often individuals have not considered the other relationships in terms of their own school and where they fall on the continuum.

Part of our orientation of teachers to coaching was a 1-day workshop with Stephen Barkley in which teachers asked themselves where on the relationship continuum their school staff fell and set goals about where they would like to be in the future. Most felt they were in the "congenial" range—and had never considered that although this is a phase necessary to moving on to deeper professional relationships, it can also be a place where faculties get stuck. In an effort to be socially liked or accepted, teachers may avoid topics that bring conflict. They may prefer to "do their own thing" and not make waves among their peers. This isolation can lead to a neglect of powerful conversations about practice and student achievement.

Teachers can investigate the idea that *transactive memory* can take place in professional as well as personal relationships. Studies have shown that the understandings and knowledge of the group can be higher than that of any individual member and that work groups can develop a division of cognitive labor (Hollingshead, 2000). Gladwell (2002) describes *transactive memory* as "knowing someone well enough to know what they know, and knowing them well enough so that you can trust them to know things in their specialty. It's the re-creation, on an organization-wide level, of the kind of intimacy and trust that exists in a family" (p. 190).

This can be a "sticky" idea. I don't know about your family, but mine does not always agree. When we disagree, we rarely just smile, ask about the weather, and then go in our rooms and shut the door gently. We know at some primal level we need each other to survive as a unit. We have different ideas, perspectives, and specialties, and we need each other even when we don't agree or even (gulp) like each other! But over time and through conflict, we know we can trust each other and we know to whom we can turn for what.

Starting with student achievement, our teachers worked with author and consultant Stephen Barkley on a backward mapping project beginning with the question, "What changes need to happen in student behavior and effort to get the academic improvement we want?" Then, they stepped back and considered what changes in the behavior of the adults in the building were required to elicit the student behaviors that would lead to achievement. They then evaluated the behavior changes on the part of the parents and administrators that would get them closer to their goal. Finally, they looked at what *they* could do to influence those changes. This leads teachers to not only want change to occur but also see a path to actually making that change. Instead of saying "I want to teach Johnny to learn to multiply fractions," the question becomes "I want to identify some strategies I can use that will lead to the behavior of Johnny multiplying fractions." What the teachers are doing here is identifying what Patterson and colleagues (2008) called "vital behaviors." Coaches can watch teacher practice, watch Johnny, and give the teacher feedback on when Johnny is getting it and what the teacher is doing when Johnny does get it.

After a day or two of grappling with Barth's (2006) model of teacher relationships, Knight's (2007) definition of instructional coaching and Barkley's (2010) backward mapping, explanation of the role of the coach, and definition of the purpose of coaching, our teachers were overwhelmingly positive and excited about working with a coach. When asked to reflect on their future plans, they wanted to "work more as a team" and "make an appointment with my coach to observe my teaching." One teacher wanted to "encourage my fellow teachers to be vulnerable and let the coach come in!"

Provide the Appropriate Environment for Coaching

The first day of a new job is always difficult, and the first day can make a huge difference in the attitude of the coach toward the school and the school toward the coach. When my second child was born, I had spent months preparing my older one for the new arrival—as a mother I knew instinctively that the new arrival might not be received with as much joy on the part of the sibling as that of the parents! The same is true for any new faculty member in a school. Everyone will look to the leadership in the school to see how they should react to the change, and in this instance, actions speak louder than words. An issue brief from the Center for Comprehensive School Reform and Improvement (2007) states,

> Administrators who are transparent about the purposes of the coaching program, who provide clear support for the initiative, and who indicate through their words and actions that the initiative represents a long-term commitment of human and financial resources are more likely to reassure staff members who are committed to improvement. (p. 5)

Administrators communicate their priorities by the resources they provide. The space you assign to an activity is one of the most important decisions you will make. If a coach shows up and you escort her to the broom closet to work, it will communicate to the staff that her role is unimportant, whether you mean to do this or not. A corner office with a big executive chair is probably not the right spot, either, because it could give a message that the coach is a boss. Nor should the coach be a nomad. Yes, she will be in classrooms most of the day, working with teachers, but she will also need a space for one-on-one and small-group discussion, as well as her own desk area to keep records and do paperwork.

When new schools are designed, cafeterias, libraries, and gymnasiums often are well appointed and attractive. Space for teacher collaboration and work must be convenient and attractive as well. In a perfect world, this might include a professional library, a place for the coach to research and to confer with teachers, and a large area for groups of teachers to work together. If this is not possible (and it often is not), you should evaluate the usage of current space and reassign it as necessary. It might mean that a part of the library, teacher workroom, conference room, or even the stage can be repurposed for collaboration. If we are trying to set coaching in the context of a culture of collaboration, it is our opinion that the coach should be set in a *place* for collaboration. This is often an ideal place for the coach's office—in or near the place where teachers collaborate.

Recently, someone told me she wanted to be a professional dancer but could never find the time to pursue it. It occurred to me that professional dancers are not people who "found" the time— they made the time by making it a priority in their lives. Collegiality is no different. If a coaching program is begun in a school but no time is provided to implement it, it tells the staff that coaching is not important. We "find" the time to have lunch every day, to call the roll, to make announcements. Schedules must be adjusted to allow for pre- and postobservation conferences and professional learning communities. This time—at least 90 minutes to 120 minutes a week—should be allocated during the teacher's work day. Barkley (2010) identifies several creative ways schools have done this, and we have seen many more in schools with which we have worked. Some ideas include weekly "late start" or "early dismissal" days in which all teachers have an extra hour to collaborate and the children arrive an hour later or leave an hour earlier. Other schools use teaming and create larger groups of students taught by several teachers and free up other teachers to work together. Involving all the staff in the building (counselors, librarians, administrators, etc.) allowed for a creative schedule that gave all teachers additional time to work together. Of course, substitute teachers can also be enlisted for short periods to allow for PLCs or conferencing, and coaches themselves can take on a class and practice a model lesson while the teacher is meeting with his colleagues. Common planning times for grade groups in elementary and subject areas or clusters are relatively easy ways to provide time for professional learning communities. The principal must take the leadership role in providing teachers with the flexibility to pursue their ideas for scheduling collaborative time.

We have already discussed the responsibility of the principal and coaching champion to protect the role of the coach from encroaching outside responsibilities and closely monitor the amount of time a coach can actually spend coaching. The staff must, from the start, hear from the principal that while it may be tempting to use an extra pair of hands to take on other duties from time to time, the coach must have adequate time to work with individual teachers and teacher teams to meet the long-term goal of maximum teacher capacity. Otherwise, teachers and other administrators may misinterpret the situation when a coach declines such an assignment. The principal must also clearly define and differentiate the roles and responsibilities of the coach and other support personnel in the building. Many schools with coaches have multiple resources—coaches, reading specialists, counselors, family–school coordinators, curriculum specialists—and it can be confusing for the staff when jobs seem to overlap. It can be helpful to create a "Who You Gonna Call?" sheet that includes the names of support staff and examples of the issues they address. A discussion with all support personnel in a group will be helpful to delineating responsibilities and setting up procedures for working together. We have found it helpful for mentors, coaches, Title One teachers, and reading specialists to form their own PLC so they can work together instead of competitively. Again, the key is building trust and providing transparency among the faculty. This group can also provide an emotional support network for coaches within a building. Perhaps among your more experienced staff, you can find an individual who can serve as a mentor for the coach.

Perfect Storms

A boatswain has to be ready for emergencies. Sometimes coaching happens almost like an emergency—it is pushed upon a staff quickly and urgently, and there is little time to "get it right" before it begins. Sometimes leaders step into a situation in which a coaching program has been in place for years and is ineffective. We speak to people all the time who started a coaching program, and it very quickly became an extra level of administration in a school instead of instructional coaching. Others have hired coaches who have ended up tutoring kids instead of working with teachers. Sometimes a powerful group within a school or district actively worked to sabotage a coaching program. Sometimes the coaches themselves have caused strife within a school community. Personnel or placement changes may have to occur. In these situations, we have to always go back to our vision and our values. We believe in the professionalism of teachers and the collective capacity of a group of highly skilled and talented individuals. We believe that all kids can learn and that our practice can lead to that result. When that remains the focus and we face it with courage and honesty, we can weather any storm.

Summary

When beginning an instructional coaching program, it is very important to lay the groundwork with the school level staff so that they are open and receptive to coaching. To do this,

1. Start by enrolling the support of the teacher leaders in your building.

2. Develop mini-champions among the staff—people who will help champion and support the coaches.

3. Help the staff connect coaching to their school and personal vision.

4. Accept resistance.

5. Hone the coaching message by using "sticky ideas" and powerful stories.

6. Pursue a culture of collegiality.

7. Set up a positive environment for the coach by providing physical space, time, and resources for the coach.

8. Be ready to weather the storms that may come.

If you have ever stood on a dock watching a ship from far away, everything seems to glide effortlessly across the water. Up close is a very different story. Most things that seem easy are not! Recognizing that in the real world, any worthwhile human endeavor is messy and complicated will help you gather all your forces to embark on a successful coaching voyage.

"Life uses messes to get to well-ordered solutions. Life doesn't seem to share our desires for efficiency or neatness. It uses redundancy, fuzziness, dense webs of relationships, and unending trials and errors to find what works."

—Margaret J. Wheatley and
Myron Kellner-Rogers (1999a, p. 13)

Building an Instructional Coaching Program for Maximum Capacity

1. Research coaching and coaching models. Reach out to others (coaches, coaching champions) in the professional community. (Chapter 1)

2. Select a "champion team" who will develop the coaching initiative and will support coaching. (Chapter 2)

3. Develop a shared vision of instructional coaching for your school or district. (Chapter 2)

4. Align your vision of instructional coaching with your school or district's vision. (Chapter 2)

5. Develop an administrative model for coaching. (Chapter 2)

6. Develop your assessment plan for the coaching initiative. Know what you will evaluate and how you will do it. (Chapter 3)

7. Know the five characteristics of great coaches prior to hiring and assigning, and use them to develop a recruitment strategy. Interview and hire coaches. (Chapter 4)

8. Determine preservice training needs for administrators and supervisors and develop a learning plan. (Chapter 5)

9. Determine preservice training needs for newly hired instructional coaches and develop a learning plan for the first of the school year as part of a long-term comprehensive model of ongoing professional learning and support. (Chapter 6)

10. Plan for opportunities for regular collaboration among and between coaches and teachers after coaches begin. (Chapter 7)

11. **Develop a model of ongoing learning and support for instructional coaches. (Chapter 8)**

12. Evaluate your coaching program and make necessary adjustments to sustain, change, abandon, or reimagine your coaching initiative. (Chapters 3 and 9)

8

Trimming the Sails

Ongoing Professional Learning and Support

> "The pessimist complains about the wind; the optimist expects it to change; the realist adjusts the sails."
>
> —St. Peter (2010, p. 460)

Trimming the sails is all about adjusting the tautness of the sails to the speed and direction of the wind in order to move the ship along at your desired clip, or speed. The sails have to be pulled just tightly enough to catch the wind and move the boat forward. If the sails are pulled too tightly, the boat stalls. If the sails are not pulled tightly enough, they luff (or flap loosely), causing the boat to lose speed and direction. We can apply this concept to our instructional coaching program. Once we release the newly prepared instructional coaches to the open waters of schools and classrooms, we need to constantly trim the sails of learning and support for them—too much support smothers, or stalls their progress, while too little support causes them to flounder about aimlessly. We have to provide coaches with the right balance of ongoing learning and support that allows them to assume their roles with confidence and courage.

Friday Focus and Sí C-C

It is an established fact that for professional learning to be effective, it must be sustained, intensive, ongoing, and connected to practice (Darling-Hammond, 2005; Darling-Hammond, Wei, Andree, Richardson, & Orphanos, 2009; Guskey & Yoon, 2009). One of the ways we provide ongoing support and sustained learning for our instructional coaches is through the use of regularly scheduled meetings, which we dubbed Friday Focus. Initially, we met with coaches on a weekly basis, reducing the frequency of our meetings to biweekly as the coaches grew more confident and competent in their roles and as teacher demands for their services increased. For each Friday Focus meeting, we ask coaches to report any celebrations, concerns, requests, ideas worth sharing, and questions in advance, and we use their input to develop the meeting agendas. Our coaches look forward to Friday Focus meetings because of the opportunity to learn from each other. There is usually a time during the meetings for coaches to demonstrate, model, or describe a coaching protocol or activity they have used with success. Coaches also discuss new teaching strategies they have observed during their classroom observations.

In addition, we use the time set aside for Friday Focus to reflect on general coaching praxis. In their 2009 article synthesizing research on effective professional development practices, Guskey and Yoon stress that "educators at all levels need just-in-time, job-embedded assistance as they struggle to adapt new curricula and new instructional practices to their unique classroom contexts" (p. 498). Coaches observe, model, coplan, coteach, provide resources, and consult with teachers regarding instructional practices and curriculum content. As coaching champions, we provide coaches the just-in-time learning to support their work with teachers. We might select a relevant journal article to jigsaw or a gallery walk of essential coaching habits to discuss, or we may focus on specific curriculum agendas we expect them to advance. As coaches of coaches, we look for ways to provide professional learning opportunities to sharpen their skills and increase their confidence.

Periodically, we work through an exercise we call Consulting the Compass, in which we spend time reviewing the vision and goals for the instructional coaching program and complete a self-progress check, both for individual coaches and for the coaching program as a whole. Consulting the Compass is a great focusing tool for monitoring progress and staying on target.

We also arrange regular meetings between the coaches and their respective instructional coordinators—meetings we simply call Sí C-C to reflect the "yes" or "can-do" attitude of the coaches and coordinators working together. Elementary coaches meet with the elementary-level coordinators, middle school coaches meet with the middle school coordinators, and so on. One of the purposes of these meetings is to keep everyone informed and abreast of current happenings and concerns. However, these meetings are not simply about sharing information. Many times, the instructional coordinators will have a new protocol to model or an article they have read that resonates with what coaches do or encounter. The coordinators serve as in-house experts and mentors—adding another layer of support for the coaches and the coaching program.

> **REFLECT:**   How would you construct ongoing learning opportunities with your instructional coaches to blend information sharing and professional learning? How often would you want these meetings to occur? Who will be responsible for planning and facilitating these meetings?

Consultants

Just as coaches cannot be expected to be experts in all things, coaching champions sometimes have to rely on the prowess of others to facilitate professional learning activities. When we recognize the need for targeted instruction beyond our experience and know-how, we turn to outside consultants. The consultant may be someone from the field of coaching, or he or she may be a content area expert who works with coaches to deepen their understanding of standards, to teach new strategies, or to examine the effectiveness of classroom environments. "Consultant" does not have to be synonymous with "expensive." In our state, many of our colleagues at the State Board of Education make themselves available to provide specific instruction in assessment and evaluation, curriculum changes and updates, and technology use and integration. Local universities often have professors who are willing to provide services free of charge as part of their service to the community, and nonprofits sometimes provide consulting to schools. We have also been fortunate to establish ongoing consultation arrangements with experts in the fields of mathematics and literacy who go into actual classrooms to teach and model strategies while our coaches observe. After spending time in the schools, the consultants meet with coaches to reflect on their observations, answer questions, and deepen the coaches' understanding of the new content or strategies. By including outside consultants in this way, our coaches are able to strengthen and expand their repertoire of coaching moves to use with teachers.

> **REFLECT:** Who are the in-house experts or outside consultants that can best support your coaches' learning needs or the needs of your district?

Technology Training

We also support coaches in their understanding and use of technology. Our instructional technology specialist and other technology support personnel work with coaches on an as-needed basis either individually, in small groups, or as a whole group. If a school purchases a new technology, the technology specialist offers professional learning to coaches to help them support teachers as they begin to integrate the new technology into their curricula. Furthermore, the technology specialist and support personnel share websites, software applications, blogs, newsletters, and other technology tools with coaches, equipping them with the necessary knowledge and skills to provide daily assistance and reinforcement to teachers.

We understand the budgetary and resource challenges many school districts are facing in our current economy and encourage an in-depth assessment of the collective capacity within your school and district leadership for planning and delivering learning opportunities for your coaches.

Coach the Coach

One of the most helpful supports comes from coaches coaching each other. Initially, we designed a formal plan for coaches to partner with each other in a coach-the-coach assignment. Coaches were required to draw names for this assignment in order to randomly pair coaches who were not close friends or former teaching colleagues from the same school. Coaches were given about 4 weeks to schedule a time to complete a complete coaching cycle (preconference, observation, reflecting conference) with a teacher in their schools. Each coach was required to videotape the pre- and postconference with the teacher. Then, the first coach's partner would view the videoed conferences and conduct a coaching conference with the coach—discussing the strengths and challenges of the first coach's conferencing skills. Once coaches completed this formal assignment as both observer and the one being observed, they spent time during Friday Focus sharing their experiences. This support provided a springboard for coaches to be more vulnerable with each other, and they began asking for coaching feedback from their peers on a regular basis—with no directive from their coaching champions to do so.

Conferences

As might be expected, we foster coaches and their learning by taking or sending them to conferences. It is often much more cost effective to send a team of coaches to a conference and ask them to share what they learned with other coaches who, in turn, can share with teachers in every school, than it is to send someone from every school. Each school or district will have to decide which conferences will be the most helpful for your coaches to attend. Our coaches have attended state- and national-level conferences for leadership; technology; reading; mathematics; science; STEM (science, technology, engineering, and math);

and coaching. Regardless of how many coaches actually attend a particular conference, all coaches receive information from the conferences that they can share with teachers and administrators in their schools. A bonus from sending our coaches to several different conferences is the inspiration many of them received that motivated them to seek out opportunities to present at both state and national conferences. If it is true that "he who teaches learns the most," then a number of our coaches are set to take some giant steps in their own learning!

Site Visits

Site visits can serve a multitude of purposes, but the constant, underlying purpose is to demonstrate support for the instructional coach and/or the coaching program. As coaching champions, we want to observe firsthand the kinds of coaching activities our coaches and teachers are involved in. The best way to accomplish this is to visit the schools. During our site visits, we conferred with principals and coaches, and we observed coaches leading Socratic seminars, teaching strategies, facilitating professional learning communities, conferencing with individual teachers, and leading professional development activities. Site visits have given us the privilege to see the growth our coaches are experiencing and to see the impact they are having with teachers. Site visits allow for those informal conversations with administrators that serve as good reminders that coaching champions work to support all aspects of coaching and the coaching program, including support for administrators as they work toward full implementation of the coaching program. One of the best reasons we have found for site visits comes at the invitation of the coaches, who may ask us to observe something special they are doing with a faculty or who may just want a few minutes to be coached themselves.

Coaching Academy Partnership

Perhaps one of the most extensive plans we developed for ongoing professional learning and support for coaches was a joint venture with a local university to create a weeklong coaching academy during the summer. Working with the dean and the associate dean of the university's College of Education, we designed a comprehensive menu of leadership topics tailored to meet our coaches' specific professional learning needs. The collaborative planning process took several months, as the dean wanted to make optional graduate credit available to coaches who completed the academy. In the end, our coaches participated in more than 40 hours of professional learning during the academy. In preparation for the academy, we required all coaches to read, as a joint book study, Pink's *A Whole New Mind* (2005). The coaching champions prepared visual summaries (PechaKuchas) of Collins's *Good to Great* (2001) and Gladwell's *Outliers* (2008) and designed small-group activities for coaches to discuss.

The coaching academy proved to be a phenomenal learning and growth opportunity for coaches and coaching champions alike. The carefully designed learning schedule included topics such as leadership, balance, communication skills, the adult learner, conflict resolution, change theory, and qualities of effective presentations. The academy leaders engaged participants through role-play, games, discussions, readings, case studies and scenarios, and listening and reflecting activities. Each day included time for group discussion, reflection, and application to each participant's unique coaching situation. This endeavor proved to be a very cost effective way to provide targeted learning for all our coaches and champions in a brief period.

> **REFLECT:** Think about approaching a local university or college to enlist them as partners in developing a coaching academy for your coaches. Who needs to be involved? What kind of budget do you have for such an endeavor? What would be the targeted learning goals for your coaches? Would you open the academy to school leaders as well?

Relationship

We first learned of the *new* 3 Rs—rigor, relevance, and relationship—at an International Model Schools Conference we attended several years ago in Washington, D.C. The 3 Rs address the key characteristics of effective classrooms. For us, those same 3 Rs—rigor, relevance, and relationship—are also key characteristics of successful coaching programs.

As coaching facilitators for a new instructional coaching program, we knew our coaches would experience rigor as they met the challenges that any new change initiative brings. We also felt confident that the coaching program would prove relevant for all stakeholders because we had been so careful to align the program to support our district vision and goals, and because coaching speaks to the heart of teaching and learning. Moreover, we knew we had selected a team of coaches who came with proven track records for establishing and maintaining positive relationships with colleagues, parents, students, and supervisors. What we as coaching champions had to be mindful of was the importance of developing genuine, caring, and supportive relationships between the coaches and their coaching champions.

The coach–coaching champion relationship is not so much about being friends, although friendships can easily develop between coaches and coaching champions. The relationship is more like the one that exists between a servant leader and her faculty. Regardless of the number of different hats we wear during the day, we must find (sometimes create) time in our schedules to listen, respond, intervene, advise, congratulate, advocate, laugh, and occasionally worry or even grieve with our coaches. The relationship between coach and coaching champion is the kind of ongoing support that probably gets the least attention in the world of coaching but makes the greatest difference in coaches' morale, confidence, and determination to succeed.

There are many ways to build positive relationships with those we supervise. One of the amazing traits among teachers and coaches is their heartfelt gratitude for expressions of approval, appreciation, and acknowledgment from their supervisors. While corporate climbers compete for huge salary bonuses, coaches and teachers are thrilled to hear words of thanks, whether in the form of a verbal "Thank you," an e-mail or handwritten note, or a private or public acknowledgment for work well done or an excellent idea. One of the most important components in the coach–champion relationship is the mutual respect that comes from working side by side as colleagues striving for the same goals. Coaching champions must continually demonstrate that respect through listening to and supporting the ideas and initiatives of the coaches.

REFLECT: How prepared are you to support your coaches through relationship? Is this an area of strength for you or is it an area of challenge? If relationship is an area of strength, how can you leverage this strength on behalf of your coaches? If relationship is an area of challenge, what steps can you take to strengthen this essential leadership quality?

Summary

1. Provide the right balance of ongoing learning and support in order for coaches to build confidence, courage, and capacity.

2. Plan regularly scheduled meetings between coaches and their coaching champions to give coaches the opportunity to share and learn.

3. Enlist the assistance of instructional coordinators to meet regularly with coaches for information sharing, learning, and mentoring.

4. When necessary (and feasible), contract with outside consultants who can bring new experiences to coaches and teachers.

5. Arrange formal coach-the-coach observations for coaches to support each other in their praxis.

6. Identify state and national conferences that support your district's needs and send some or all of your coaches.

7. Visit coaches where they work as a strong demonstration of support and encouragement.

8. Consider working with a local college or university to develop a coaching academy tailored to meet the needs of your coaches.

9. Take time to do the important work of building relationships with your coaches.

By trimming the sails with ongoing professional learning and support, we build individual and collective capacity to enable our instructional coaches to proceed with the necessary confidence, skills, and courage to take teachers to the shores of excellence and distinction.

Building an Instructional Coaching Program for Maximum Capacity

1. Research coaching and coaching models. Reach out to others (coaches, coaching champions) in the professional community. (Chapter 1)

2. Select a "champion team" who will develop the coaching initiative and will support coaching. (Chapter 2)

3. Develop a shared vision of instructional coaching for your school or district. (Chapter 2)

4. Align your vision of instructional coaching with your school or district's vision. (Chapter 2)

5. Develop an administrative model for coaching. (Chapter 2)

6. Develop your assessment plan for the coaching initiative. Know what you will evaluate and how you will do it. (Chapter 3)

7. Know the five characteristics of great coaches prior to hiring and assigning, and use them to develop a recruitment strategy. Interview and hire coaches. (Chapter 4)

8. Determine preservice training needs for administrators and supervisors and develop a learning plan. (Chapter 5)

9. Determine preservice training needs for newly hired instructional coaches and develop a learning plan for the first of the school year as part of a long-term comprehensive model of ongoing professional learning and support. (Chapter 6)

10. Plan for opportunities for regular collaboration among and between coaches and teachers after coaches begin. (Chapter 7)

11. Develop a model of ongoing learning and support for instructional coaches. (Chapter 8)

12. Evaluate your coaching program and make necessary adjustments to sustain, change, abandon, or reimagine your coaching initiative. (Chapters 3 and 9)

9

Mooring the Ship

Avalon or Ithaca?

If developing a coaching program is like a sea voyage, at some point you would expect to arrive at your destination. Let's face it: We would all like to reach the destination of instructional coaching with a sense of accomplishment. The question is, when you reach it, will you find mythical Avalon or real-life Ithaca?

In the legend of King Arthur, Avalon is the mystical place where Arthur received Excalibur and where he returned at the end of his life to return the sword. It is a beautiful place, inhabited by magical women, where "no wind blows and where hail, rain and snow have never been known to fall" (Manguel & Guadalupi, 2000, p. 47). In Celtic mythology, Avalon is like the Garden of Eden—it is a place where you do not have to farm the land. The environment simply provides everything you need to survive.

Ithaca is a real island in the Ionic Sea, in contrast to some of the other locations in Homer's *Odyssey*. Ithaca is the home to which Odysseus returns after his life of adventure sailing around the seas, fighting Cyclopes, and avoiding Lotus Eaters. In contrast to Avalon, things were not going so well in Ithaca when Odysseus returned. While he was away, a band of suitors had arrived to steal away his wife and his wealth. To get back his rightful place in the family, he had to pass a test of skill and strength, woo back his wife, kill the suitors, and hang the treacherous maids. Odysseus was almost killed himself, but the goddess Athena intervened and saved him. In Ithaca, everything does not take care of itself.

Avalon is perfect, but Ithaca is a real place, with all its flaws. Likewise, teaching and learning are messy human endeavors that will never reach perfection and will always defy exacting implementation. The goal, then, is to create a school culture in which change and continual improvement are the norm, and risk taking is encouraged. Coaching is one way to do this, but it must be in concert with a whole culture and structure of growth. At the end of one cycle of implementation, the next cycle begins—reevaluation, realignment, and reimplementation. How then do you monitor and sustain your coaching program in light of the unforeseen promise and possibilities of the future? What do we do when unforeseen events require us to change course midstream?

> *"We must free ourselves of the hope that the sea will ever rest. We must learn to sail in high winds."*
>
> —Aristotle Onassis

I used to say that raising children was like "trying to fill a bucket with a hole in it; you never really get finished," and most other important human endeavors are the same—including improvement of any sort. The goal of this book is to help you get to the point at which you have a viable coaching initiative in place. We would be remiss, however, if we left the impression that getting to that point is anything other than the beginning of your journey.

Study and Respond to Your Results

Previously, we looked at formative assessment practices that can help you improve your program, your coaches, your administrative support, and your developing collaborative relationships. This cycle of formative assessment continues as your program grows and changes. At some point, you will have to make decisions about expanding, changing, or ending a coaching program, and you will want to know if the resources you are putting into the program justify the results. For these purposes, you will need to know if teachers are using coaching, and if they are, whether their practice has been impacted positively so that students will benefit. Coaches' records should be compared to teacher's self-reporting to determine the number and quality of coaching interactions that are taking place. Teachers and administrators should be surveyed and interviewed concerning both the coaching interactions and the overall levels of collaboration in a building. This should be done annually to identify trends. Principals and other instructional leaders should do follow-up observations to see that teachers are in fact implementing the pedagogy and content that they were to have worked on with the coach. Finally, student performance data from a variety of measures (including benchmarking data) should be evaluated. In some cases, you can find statistically similar schools at which coaching did not take place and evaluate gains in terms of this comparison. This data should be reviewed by administrators, teachers, and coaching champions, and perhaps other district personnel as well. Ultimately however, it will fall to the leader of the program or school to make hard decisions about next steps.

Drucker and colleagues (2008) identify one of the most important questions you can ask about your organization: "What are our results?" In a school or other nonprofit environment, this is an especially important question, because resources are limited and the mission is important. A heavy force against looking at results is the personal attachment individuals and organizations feel toward programs and personnel that are ineffective. It is much easier to start a new program than to end an ineffective program. For this reason, it is helpful to look not only at the results from your coaching program but also at the results of other kinds of professional development and classroom support in which you may still be investing. Is coaching working better than these other programs? If so, is it possible to shift resources to the initiatives that work best? The answer to the question "What are our results?" will lead you to expand, sustain, change, or abandon coaching.

Expand Your Program

You may find that the program is so successful that people are yearning for more. Places where some form of coaching or collaborative professional learning is already in place often consider hiring more coaches or expanding coaches. Mangin (2009) studied 20 school districts considering hiring literacy coaches. Districts with PLCs or in which reading specialists had acted as coaches were more likely to implement literacy coaching. In our experience, in schools in which part-time coaching had been exceptionally effective, principals requested full-time dedicated coaches in their buildings.

Faced with success, you will need to discover ways to feed the ever-increasing need to grow professionally on the part of your coaches and teachers, and you will continue to hire, train, and support additional coaches. If resources are available, this is an exhilarating challenge. Our coaching program was very successful in our first year. This led to a desire for a new and different layer of coaches to focus on math instruction the second year. This time, our job seemed easier in many ways. We did not have to put nearly as much effort into explaining what coaching was to teachers, applicants for the positions, or building-level administrators. However, this "second generation" of coaches did not always get the intentional professional learning and support they needed as we all became more comfortable in our roles. The challenge in this case is to continually build the capacity of your coaches by frequent checking-in procedures to find out how the coaches, principals, and teachers are feeling about their practice and by providing the ongoing professional development they need to grow.

In some places, instructional coaching has become so effective that it has led to a change in the evaluation system of teachers. In Walton High School, Marietta, Georgia, teachers were given the option of working with a peer coach over the course of the year instead of going through a typical evaluation cycle with an administrator (Barkley, 2010). These teachers received peer coaching and professional learning, identified a specific focus for improvement, and, at the end of the cycle, held a conference with their principal to discuss ways they had grown and improved on that focus area over the year.

Sustain Your Program

Sometimes coaching programs are attacked as too expensive to maintain, and you may find yourself struggling to sustain a program financially even though the data are showing success. In a system of year-to-year evaluation and the need to achieve NCLB annual benchmarks in order to remain a viable school, some decision makers become shortsighted and insist on using all available resources to help the children "just pass the test this year." Building long-term capacity takes a back seat to making it through the spring testing season. In a time in which administrators' and teachers' jobs can hang on the balance of one year's test scores, this is not an unreasonable tactic, but it is a shortsighted one. With a shift in viewpoint, coaching can actually be a more cost-effective way to reach more students. In a study by Mangin (2009), some school systems maximized their collective capacity to reach students by shifting funds away from professional staff developers and toward school-embedded professional learning that included observing and engaging in critical conversations about practice. With more and more students underachieving, it seemed more efficient to hire coaches to work with teachers to improve their literacy instruction than to hire more paraprofessionals or reading specialists to work one on one with students. These schools embraced the concept that "when coaches help teachers reach their students, they help every student teachers will teach for the rest of their lives" (Knight, 2011, p. 99).

Professional development has historically been expensive. In 2000, Miles and Hornbeck (as cited in Knight, 2011) found four urban districts that spent $2,010 to $6,628 per teacher on professional development. It makes sense to reallocate some of these funds to a professional development model that has been shown to be more effective in improving instruction than the traditional workshop model. This shift is not easy, however, because our old practices and policies become ingrained in our organizational culture, budgeting system, policies, and procedures. Current imperatives call us to think outside of the box on those issues, however.

Abandoning programs and strategies can be as important as creating new ones. Sometimes, in order to sustain instructional coaching, you must abandon other programs that may be good but do not get you closer to your mission and vision. As Drucker et al. (2008) pointed out, need and tradition are not strong enough factors to keep an organization tied to a plan or program. That program must match both the mission and results. In Mangin's (2009) study, districts that wished to change to a job-embedded instructional coaching model of professional development were reluctant to eliminate programs in order to create others. While some wished to transform the job categories of reading specialists and paraprofessionals into coaching positions, this was difficult because these individuals were "deeply institutionalized members of the school and local communities." Teachers relied on these professionals and paraprofessionals to work with the individual students who needed extra assistance. In districts that adopted coaching, the paradigm shifted to one of collective responsibility in which "teachers were viewed as sharing responsibility for all students" (Mangin 2009, p. 2). In many cases, reading specialists can be retrained to act as literacy or instructional coaches in a building, but in others, the person is not a good fit for this kind of position, and this brings a human relationship dilemma for many leaders. We have to make our choices, no matter how difficult, based on what is best for the students and not just the adults in the building. Drucker (2008) suggests we should ask of any program, "If we were not committed to this today, would we go into it?" If the answer is negative, we have to ask, "How can we get out—fast?" (p. 68).

Change Your Program

I was recently reading a passage in a book about the seafaring Maoris (the indigenous people of Oceania) when I came upon this sentence: "Some settlements were the result of accidental voyages but others, of planned migrations in fleets of large canoes" (*The Last 1000 Years*, 1999, p. 55). It occurred to me that sometimes we arrive in a big fleet for a planned migration, but often the best things that happen in schools or life are the result of "accidental voyages." When creative changes in a program are necessary due to limited resources, we sometimes end up with a settlement all the same.

In our study and our experience, every school should have clear goals and effective professional learning communities in which fierce conversations about practice and student achievement occur daily. Ideally, to facilitate this culture, every school would have one or more coaches whose primary goals are helping teachers celebrate successes, expand their repertoire of instructional strategies, and reflect on their professional practice. Sometimes we cannot have the ideal situation in the short term. In the face of hard economic or political realities, many systems have had to seriously limit their coaching programs.

When we began a coaching program, our district did not have enough money to hire the number of coaches we wanted—one per school. Since our short-term goal was to introduce our whole district to this practice, we opted to assign multiple schools—as many as four—to some coaches. Over time, you may wish to go back and focus your resources where they can make the most impact. Coaches can be assigned at schools with the highest poverty levels or the lowest test scores. In making this decision, however, it is important to survey how much the school wants coaching. If the resources are limited, the place where coaches will be used the most is where they should be placed. The bottom line is to ask yourself, "What is best for the students in our school district? Where will coaches have the greatest impact?" You may also wish to consider the content areas that you wish to focus on. If your goal is to improve math achievement, you might wish to place instructional coaches only with math teachers at the secondary level, for example. In some programs, changing priorities mean changing the role or type of coach. You may have to reorganize your coaching program to move toward data coaches to fulfill accountability needs, for example, and leave some of the instructional coaching to a peer program.

Another way to increase coaching capacity is to use coaches as "coaches of peer coaches." Our district spent a considerable amount of money training our coaches in coaching strategies. This resource is a valuable one. These trained coaches can in turn train peer coaches in every school to sustain the coaching momentum. Clary, Oglan, and Styslinger (2008) reported on a secondary school program called Project RAISSE (Reading Assistance Initiative for Secondary School Educators). In this model, content area teachers were trained to be literacy coaches in their buildings. They received 6 hours of graduate credit for their professional learning and then were expected to facilitate collegial study groups in their schools. The program was so popular, eventually the principal moved to expand it to all teachers in the school. A district that already has instructional coaches could use a similar model using coaches to train a cadre of teachers to be peer coaches each year and could then coach the coaches in their practice.

Other districts have a part-time coaching model in which a coach teaches for part of the day. This model could be easier to implement in secondary schools in which teachers can have a designated period or two for coaching. Schools would have to evaluate and adapt their schedule structure so that coaches would have time to work with different teachers at different times of the day. This is an obstacle, but one that can be creatively handled. Coaches may job share with another teacher who only wants to work part of a day or a few days a week, or a coach—perhaps a retiree—may be willing to coach part time.

In the absence of a full-time coach, another suggestion is to implement one-on-one collegial coaching in which teachers submit proposals to a leadership team and are then chosen to receive coaching from a colleague. The two teachers get professional learning in coaching practices and then coach each other on an identified strategy (Brozo & Fisher, 2010). If your coaching force is seriously curtailed due to limited funding, this may also be a way to continue coaching in many schools with only a few coaches. Coaches could visit schools and help them implement their own collegial coaching interactions.

One concern that you will want to address as your coaching program matures and you make decisions about the future is the length of time a coach should be away from full-time teaching. In the absence of good data on that question, it is our opinion that it depends upon the circumstance and upon the coach. On one hand, a well-trained and experienced coach is a resource that should be leveraged. On the other, a coach who is too long outside the classroom may begin to lose her focus or her credibility with teachers. Although coaches are in the classroom every day, perhaps even modeling lessons, they do not have to handle the same issues with parents, grading, and discipline issues that classroom teachers do. Often coaches simply miss the classroom and are anxious to try new strategies with students of their own. This phenomenon is no different than what can occur with administrators, district supervisors, or university professors, and it can be handled in several ways.

One idea is to offer your coaches a teaching sabbatical every few years. The coach will switch places with a teacher who has potential to be a coach herself. The time could be spent on professional learning for that teacher in coaching skills so that when the coach's teaching sabbatical (a semester or a year) is complete, the teacher could be a peer coach or apply for a full-time coaching position. This system has the added benefit of building your future coaching workforce.

Other coaching programs may be designed for teachers to rotate in and out of coaching in a set amount of time. In this case, it is best to keep coaches in place a minimum of 3 years. It is also advisable to stagger the rotation, so you do not have all new coaches at once in a district. If you have a cadre that can rotate in this manner, you always have coaches with experience who are in the classroom and who can be coaching supporters or champions in a school.

Abandon and Reimagine

Although in our experience and in our research, it is clear that coaching works, there are times when for some reason you must admit that the program as it has been designed is ineffective and not worth continuing. Sometimes leaders just have to admit that the first effort was ill conceived or poorly executed, and you need to go back to the starting place. Always you should go back to your vision. If you don't have a clear vision, you develop one. And then you go through the process of realigning and redefining and reimagining who you are and who you want to be as a school or district. You are honest and transparent with your staff and yourself. You conduct one or many fierce conversations. You go back and evaluate what you need to do to become the best you need to be for your team and your students. You investigate ways to approach excellence in teaching and learning in your school, and you begin again. Coaching is about second chances, and that applies to administrators and coaching champions as well.

Actualize

Ideally, coaching will be so successful that everyone will give and receive coaching as a part of the collaborative culture in which they work. Principals, teachers, students—all members of the learning community—will engage in reciprocal teaching, learning, problem solving, and reflection to increase individual and collective capacity at all levels of learning. When this happens, your culture has outgrown the structural framework of your coaching program and scaffolding is no longer necessary. The essence of capacity building is in the air—maximum capacity is within reach.

Resources

Chapter 2 Resources

SAMPLE BOOK REVIEW CHART

A chart such as the one on page 129 can be created and shared in Google Docs to keep up with your research team's reading and can also be used by coaches. Knowing who has read what saves time, and notations for future use are helpful.

Author	Title	Topic	Suggested audience	Recommendation/ purpose	Reader
Knight, Jim	*Instructional Coaching*	Coaching	Champions, coaches, principals	Overview; initial orientation	
Oczukus, Lori	*Interactive Think-Aloud Lessons*	Reading strategies	Elementary coaches	Ideas for modeling	
Pavelka, Patricia	*Differentiating Instruction in a Whole Group Setting*	Differentiation strategies	Coaches	Strategies to share	
Kise, Jane A. G.	*Differentiated Coaching: A Framework for Helping Teachers Change*	Facilitating change through coaching	Champions	Background	
Moxley, Dale, and Taylor, Rosemary	*Literacy Coaching: A Handbook for School Leaders*	Strategies	Admin staff	NM: distill into bullet points for principals	
Davis, Bonnie M.	*How to Coach Teachers Who Don't Think Like You*	Strategies	Coaches	CC: Coaches' book study	

Sample Planning Benchmarks

The following is an example of an initial planning document a coaching program planning team might create to set short-term and long-term expectations.

Focus of the Program

The teacher has the greatest impact on student learning. Instructional coaching has the potential to make good teachers great and great teachers even better!

Long-Term Expectations: End of Year 2

Coaching *is* job-embedded professional learning. We want to build *capacity* within our schools so that our teachers will have a vision of how to continue growing a collaborative culture beyond the coaching experience.

Long-Term Expectations: End of Year 1

The instructional coaching program should be a seamless, smooth-running machine in which principals, teachers, and coaches work together to affect student achievement in a positive way.

Short-Term Expectations: End of First Quarter

1. "Go slow to go fast." We want big results in a short amount of time. The adage "go slow to go fast" must be kept in mind, or we will roll right over the teachers.

2. The coaching champions will lay the groundwork for coaches to begin working with teachers in their assigned schools.

3. "Go slow to go fast" with principals, too. Meet with the principal, articulate vision for coaching as principal articulates vision for his or her school; develop a plan for the coach to meet the staff; set a few short-term goals with the principal.

4. Prepare coaches to interact with a range of perspectives and practices that are already in existence in their assigned schools. The coaches needs to orient themselves to the schools' cultures to know how to best begin initiating support within the classrooms.

SAMPLE COACH/PRINCIPAL GOALS FORM

This form can be used to articulate goals in initial meetings of principals, champions, and coaches.

School Year: _____

Name of School: _____

Goals communicated by the principal:

1.

2.

3.

Goals set by the instructional coach:

1.

2.

3.

Goals set by the content area coach:

1.

2.

3.

As you discuss these goals with your principal, consider the following:

What are your roles and responsibilities in meeting these goals?

What are your boundaries at work?

With which clients (teachers) does your principal want you to work?

What support do you need to meet the goals described?

Chapter 3 Resources

Sample Coaching Presentation Form

Coaches may be asked to document presentations to school faculties using this form.

Name of coach presenter: _____

Location of presentation: _____

Date of presentation: _____ Start time: _____ End time: _____

TOPIC of presentation: _____

Approximate number of participants: _____

(Attach sign-in sheet if available.)

CIRCLE participants' primary roles:

administrators   teachers   community members   parents
support staff   students   visiting educators

Brief description of presentation:

Please list any suggestions, comments, or concerns voiced by the participants about instructional coaching in general and/or the instructional coaching program specifically.

SAMPLE EXPECTED COACHING FOCUS

This form, based on Killion and Harrison (2006), can be used to guide coaches as they focus their work.

Fifty percent to 60% of coaching time should be spent on the following (deep) activities:*

- Pre-/postconferences
- Observations
- Coplanning lessons
- Coteaching lessons
- Data dialogues (analyzing, interpreting, discussing, informing decisions)
- Lesson study
- Modeling

Other coaching activities may include:

- District initiatives conversations
- Celebrations
- Conferences with administrators
- Coordinating with other coaches
- Personal professional development
- Professional development for staff
- Record keeping/logs
- Release time for peer teacher observations
- Resource and research assistance
- Team/department meetings

District initiatives (list your district initiatives here):

*50% to 60% equals 3.5 or more hours per day.

SAMPLE COACHING PURCHASE REQUEST FORM

This form can be used to gather information to plan a coaching program budget.

School Year: _____

This form is for budget planning purposes only. Please fill out a separate form for each item/service/professional learning/session. Consider all aspects of our program.

Person(s) making request: _____

I need this for (check one or more):

_____ A strategy that I intend to   _____ Celebration
teach/model

_____ My recordkeeping   _____ My own professional
responsibilities   learning

_____ Staff development I intend to   _____ Parent involvement
provide

_____ Materials/equipment/services/professional learning to be
shared with all coaches

Detailed description of item/service requested

_____

_____

_____

_____

_____

How would this improve instruction for students?

_____

_____

_____

_____

_____

How does this support the district or coaching mission/vision?

_____

_____

_____

_____

_____

Approximate date needed: _____

Approximate expense (if known): _____

_____

_____

_____

_____

_____

On a scale of 1 to 10, how needed is this item/service/session/professional learning? _____

_____

_____

_____

_____

_____

Please attach any supporting documentation (website, catalog page, research abstract, etc.).

Sample Recordkeeping Procedures

The following is a list of recordkeeping procedures for coaches.

Daily log and itinerary:

1. You will submit your daily log for the current week and itinerary for the following week on **FRIDAY (or the last day) of each week.**

2. **PLEASE submit electronically.**

3. Please keep a copy for yourself for your "e-portfolio."

Monthly reports:

1. These are due the last school day of each month.

2. Two forms will be turned in: one for each of your schools that lists all the teachers at that school, and one that is a summary of the totals for each school of each of the eight specific coaching activities we are following.

3. You will record the code number (1–8) in the cell corresponding to the DATES that each of the eight specific coaching activities occurred with that teacher. If you work with a group, please put the code next to **each** teacher you work with. (Sign-in sheets to Professional Learning Communities [PLCs] are helpful for this purpose and for documentation.)

4. A key at the bottom of the coaching activity spreadsheet will help you remember which of the eight codes to use. It is also at the top of the monthly summary sheet.

5. At the end of the month, tally all of your numbers and put them on the summary sheet by school. Attach the summary sheet to the top of the spreadsheets and turn in.

COACHING INTERACTION CHART

Using the key below, code the type of coaching interaction in the appropriate box.

Please indicate the date of the month in the cells below.

Teacher Name	Check if first year teacher	Indicate grade and subject taught	1	2	3	4	5	6	7	8	9	10	11	12	13	14	15	16	17	18	19	20	21	22

KEY

1 = Observation Cycle (Mark Date Complete), 2 = Coplanning (Individual Teacher), 3 = Coplanning (Team/Dept/Plc), 4 = Coteaching, 5 = Lesson Study, 6 = Modeling Lesson (Individual Teacher), 7 = Data Review (Individual Teacher), 8 = Data Review (Group)

Adapted from the NSDC Coaching Project Coaching Interaction Record.

School	1 Conferencing—observing cycle	2 Coplanning with individual teacher	3 Coplanning with team or dept. (PLC)	4 Coteaching	5 Lesson study	6 Model lessons	7 Data review with individual	8 Data review with group	9	TOTAL
1 A										
2										
3										
TOTALS										

Instructions: List each school and the **number of each type** of coaching activity conducted. Total by activity in the bottom row and by school in the last column. Staple to the top of all of your individual school's tally sheets. Please keep a copy for yourself. May be typed or written in dark pen.

Sample Log And Itinerary

This itinerary and log is used for coaches to keep up with their daily interactions and appointments and can be kept and shared electronically.

Itinerary for the week of _____   COACH NAME: _____

	Monday	Tuesday	Wednesday	Thursday	Friday	OTHER
	School:	School:	School:	School:	School:	School:
7:00						
8:00						
9:00						
10:00						
11:00						
12:00						
1:00						
2:00						
3:00						
4:00						

Log for the week of _____

COACH NAME: _____

	Monday	Tuesday	Wednesday	Thursday	Friday	OTHER
	School:	School:	School:	School:	School:	School:
7:00						
8:00						
9:00						
10:00						
11:00						
12:00						
1:00						
2:00						
3:00						
4:00						

Sample Records Communication

This letter can be used to explain the recordkeeping process to coaches.

Coaches,

Thanks so much for getting all your records in on time and in good order!

Now that you are all getting the hang of keeping these records, we wanted to remind you of their purpose.

First, you are all professionals, and we trust you to make professional choices as to how you use your time. We don't look at any logs to make judgments about you or how you are performing your job. It is just one piece of data, and we are looking at the big picture.

Second, we KNOW that not everything you do can be put into a neat category.

The coaching activities spreadsheet that you will turn in tomorrow is designed by date so YOU can look at who you are working with and look for patterns in your coaching interactions. Determine for yourself if you may be spending too much energy with one group or teacher, and then you can make your own choices (with your principal) as to how to proceed. We will not tell you to spend more or less time with someone.

We also use the Coaching Interaction form to keep very basic records about how many interactions and how many teachers are involved in the coaching program—it is quantitative, not qualitative data. We will be looking at group, not individual, data, so don't worry about comparing yourself to anyone else (we don't!). You may work with only one teacher one week, and that could be as valuable as someone else working with 10—YOU make that call, in collaboration with your principal.

We can help talk through these decisions as much as you want us too, but you know the situation better than we do . . . If you are struggling at a specific school, go back and look at your data there . . . is there something you could tweak that might make it more effective? Is there a pocket of teachers that you just can't seem to connect with? Can you pick out a person from that group that might help you be accepted by others?

The data part of that form is NOT for us to decide if you are working enough hours! It is NOT a timesheet!! You do NOT need to have 37.5 hours on that form, because some things can't be logged. There is no place for routine administrative tasks such as setting appointments, for example. We want you to use the form to see if you are working toward a goal of 50% to 60% of your time in the seven *deep* coaching activities. We don't expect you to be there yet, and we don't want you to compare yourself to others. Everyone has a different situation. Knowing that you need to spend most of your time on these activities will hopefully keep you from getting overwhelmed with requests for noncoaching duties at your schools.

We will use the data form to look at growth of the program over time—how many hours were spent on the seven *deep* coaching activities in year one and how many hours in year two, for example. It will let us know if we are on target as a group (not individuals). We will also look at how much time is spent on different district initiatives so we can see if we need to shift our emphasis!

SAMPLE E-PORTFOLIO DIRECTIONS

You may wish your coaches to keep a portfolio of their work. This is an example. Several open-source platforms (Mahara and Moodle) and others (Taskstream, LiveText) will allow you to create online portfolios that are file cabinets for all kinds of information and can be mined for data.

Purpose:

- Provide an opportunity for you to reflect on your year of coaching and identify goals for next year.
- Document coaching activities for accountability purposes.
- Share ideas and practices with each other.

Please maintain confidentiality in your reflections. This journal is for sharing!

The coaching portfolio will include the following folders:

- All daily logs and itineraries, including Individual Coaching Activities forms and one-on-one coaching and conversation monthly reports.
- Reflection journaling from at least one experience per month that was meaningful to you. This should be information that resulted in identification of strengths, challenges, ah-has, or celebrations.
- Presentation form for each professional development workshop you facilitated. (You may include a video summary of the workshop if you wish.)
- A list of each professional development workshop you attended, including conferences. (You may include your notes here if you wish.)
- Presentation PowerPoints, outlines, handouts used in workshops or teacher meetings.
- Your original model lessons or coteaching lessons.
- Photos of special projects you worked on.
- Copies of newsletters you prepared for your teachers or principals.
- Celebrations! (notes, photos, etc.)

Sample Coach Evaluation Artifacts

Every learning organization has different evaluation processes for coaches. The following is one example.

Evaluation of Coaches: Overview

The following components will be in your comprehensive evaluation experience:

- Monthly coaching data summary
- Survey of your principals
- Survey of your teachers
- E-portfolio of activities
- Two observations of your work, including the following state evaluation components:
  - Self-assessment
  - Lesson plan for a workshop, PLC, lesson study, or teacher meeting
  - Pre-/postobservation conference reflection
  - Summative evaluation and professional growth plan

Your coaching champion will conduct the observations of your workshop, PLC, lesson study session, or teacher meeting and reflect with you after they are completed. We will create a future growth plan together after a summative reflection and celebration meeting.

Chapter 4 Resources

SAMPLE CONTENT-SPECIFIC JOB DESCRIPTION

This job description can used to post coaching positions.

Job title: Instructional Coach, _____ emphasis

Supervisor: Director of Instruction

Immediate supervisor: Instructional Coaching Facilitator

Objective: To support the district's _____ teachers in the implementation of research-based strategies and curricula by demonstrating and supporting exemplary instructional practices.

Duties and Responsibilities

Work with teachers individually, in collaborative teams, and/or with departments, providing practical support on a full range of instructional strategies.

Provide ongoing support to _____ teachers in the implementation of best practices in the areas of _____ in order to support the key concepts of the discipline. Support explicit instruction of key academic vocabulary in _____ and support literacy development required to do well on _____ concepts.

Demonstrate and model exemplary instructional practices and research-based strategies for _____ teachers.

Assist teachers in reviewing student assessment data; determining appropriate interventions, modifications, and scaffolded instruction for students; and guiding teachers as needed in organizing for instruction and integrating research-based practices in the classroom.

Share best instructional practices in the teaching of _____ with teachers, administrators, and others supporting math instruction in the classroom.

Help select appropriate curriculum materials for the classroom.

Provide direction in and demonstration of classroom-management strategies as needed.

Collaborate with the special education and English Language Learner teachers in implementation of appropriate interventions and modifications in the regular education classroom.

Participate in professional development activities by attending _____ and instructional coaching workshops and conferences, reading current research and professional literature, and disseminating information gathered as a result of these activities.

Assist in providing professional development opportunities for teachers and support staff in the areas of math, literacy, vocabulary instruction, assessment, differentiation, and RTI. Provide follow-up for teachers who have participated in professional learning activities to ensure skills are implemented in the classroom.

Model technology integration into the teaching of _____.

Maintain a daily log of activities and keep up-to-date program records.

Coordinate activities with systemwide instructional personnel.

Review and interpret system- and school-level formative and summative assessment data to identify trends and needs in math and literacy.

Job Requirements

Five or more years successful experience in classroom teaching in the subject area(s) and grade groups for which he or she will serve as instructional coach.

Demonstrated experience in presentation of professional development to teachers and a deep understanding of the issues involved in working with adult learners.

Experience in school-based instructional leadership.

Experience and knowledge in the interpretation of formative and summative assessment data.

Demonstrated competence using varied technologies to support student learning.

Knowledge and experience in differentiated brain-based instructional practices.

A master's degree in education or related field.

Excellent interpersonal skills. Ability to work collaboratively with teachers, administrators, and other school personnel.

SAMPLE REFERENCE FORM

This form can be used to gather reference information for coaching applicants.

Applicant Name: _____

Your Name: _____ Position: _____

Situation in which you worked with the applicant (circle one or more):

supervisor   coworker   instructor   mentor

To the Recommender: Please rank the applicant in the following areas based on your personal observations and interactions with the applicant.

Big ideas	Descriptors	1: Limited 2: Proficient 3: Exemplary N/A	Comments/ evidence of practice
Knowledge Base	Deep knowledge base of subject matter and curriculum	____ 1 ____ 2 ____ 3 ____ N/A	
	Deep knowledge base of pedagogy and best practices	____ 1 ____ 2 ____ 3 ____ N/A	
	Gathers/interprets individual/ schoolwide data to inform teaching decisions	____ 1 ____ 2 ____ 3 ____ N/A	
	Differentiates instruction for students	____ 1 ____ 2 ____ 3 ____ N/A	
	Plans and reflects on rigorous instruction	____ 1 ____ 2 ____ 3 ____ N/A	
	Understands adult learning theory	____ 1 ____ 2 ____ 3 ____ N/A	

Big ideas	Descriptors	1: Limited 2: Proficient 3: Exemplary N/A	Comments/ evidence of practice
	Actively pursues professional development opportunities and applies learning to classroom practice	_____ 1 _____ 2 _____ 3_____ N/A	
Relationships	Trusting/ respectful relationships with peers	_____ 1 _____ 2 _____ 3_____ N/A	
	Respectful communication/ productive collaboration	_____ 1 _____ 2 _____ 3_____ N/A	
	Listening skills	_____ 1 _____ 2 _____ 3_____ N/A	
	Reflective of his/ her practice	_____ 1 _____ 2 _____ 3_____ N/A	
	Open to feedback	_____ 1 _____ 2 _____ 3_____ N/A	
	Builds on strengths to refine practice	_____ 1 _____ 2 _____ 3_____ N/A	
Presentation and Facilitation Skills	Experience in delivering professional development to large groups	_____ 1 _____ 2 _____ 3_____ N/A	
	Experience with a variety of facilitation techniques based on adult learning theory	_____ 1 _____ 2 _____ 3_____ N/A	

(Continued)

(Continued)

Big ideas	Descriptors	1: Limited 2: Proficient 3: Exemplary N/A	Comments/ evidence of practice
	Experience facilitating small-group learning, grade-level/ content/ department meetings, committee meetings, etc.	_____ 1 _____ 2 _____ 3 _____ N/A	
	Incorporates professional reading into group work	_____ 1 _____ 2 _____ 3 _____ N/A	
	Experience using a variety of data sources to inform discussions regarding student achievement	_____ 1 _____ 2 _____ 3 _____ N/A	
Professionalism	Demonstrates effective time management	_____ 1 _____ 2 _____ 3 _____ N/A	
	Demonstrates organizational skills	_____ 1 _____ 2 _____ 3 _____ N/A	
	Demonstrates fulfillment of state and district professional development requirements	_____ 1 _____ 2 _____ 3 _____ N/A	

SAMPLE INTERVIEW RUBRIC

Chapter 4 provides some sample questions in these areas, but this form can be used with any questions you devise that help you assess the imperative qualities of coaches.

Big ideas	Potential questions around	Score	Notes
Visionary	Vision of the future of education	_____1 _____ 2 _____3	
	Articulation of vision of current school or district	_____1 _____ 2 _____3	
	Personal values and their impact on role as teacher leader	_____1 _____ 2 _____3	
	Impact of professional learning on practice	_____1 _____ 2 _____3	
	Other?	_____1 _____ 2 _____3	
	Other?	_____1 _____ 2 _____3	
Courage	Tackling a complex task	_____1 _____ 2 _____3	
	Working with others who do not want to collaborate		
	Empowering and exciting management styles	_____1 _____ 2 _____3	
	Best supervisor	_____1 _____ 2 _____3	

(Continued)

(Continued)

Big ideas	Potential questions around	Score	Notes
	Other?	_____1 _____2 _____3	
	Other?	_____1 _____2 _____3	
Masterful teacher	Description of own lesson(s)	_____1 _____2 _____3	
	Description of own classroom climate	_____1 _____2 _____3	
	Description of instructional models used	_____1 _____2 _____3	
	Description of differentiation techniques	_____1 _____2 _____3	
	Description of approach to planning	_____1 _____2 _____3	
	Other?	_____1 _____2 _____3	
	Other?	_____1 _____2 _____3	
Balance	Description of challenges balancing work and personal responsibilities	_____1 _____2 _____3	
	Description of strategies to deal with stress and stressful situations	_____1 _____2 _____3	
	Description of effective time-management techniques	_____1 _____2 _____3	
	Description of organizational skills	_____1 _____2 _____3	
	Flexibility to travel and adapt schedule (if needed)	_____1 _____2 _____3	

Big ideas	Potential questions around	Score	Notes
	Other?	_____1 _____ 2 _____3	
	Other?	_____1 _____ 2 _____3	
Treasure	Contributions to current learning organization	_____1 _____ 2 _____3	
	How others (supervisors) view	_____1 _____ 2 _____3	
	How others (colleagues) view	_____1 _____ 2 _____3	
	Attitude toward current job	_____1 _____ 2 _____3	
	Desired contributions to our learning organization	_____1 _____ 2 _____3	
	Other?	_____1 _____ 2 _____3	
	Other?	_____1 _____ 2 _____3	
Arête	Passion for teaching/learning	_____1 _____ 2 _____3	
	Description of strengths	_____1 _____ 2 _____3	
	Description of weaknesses	_____1 _____ 2 _____3	
	Handling a delicate/serious situation	_____1 _____ 2 _____3	
	Professional challenges experienced	_____1 _____ 2 _____3	
	Other?	_____1 _____ 2 _____3	
	Other?		

Chapter 5 Resources

SAMPLE ORIENTATION FOR INSTRUCTIONAL COACHING

This is an example of communication with principals concerning their role in orienting new coaches to their roles.

Principals' Role

Acknowledging the role of the principal as key to the success of any instructional coaching program, we invite you to participate in the orientation process for new coaches in the following ways:

- Participate in the Principals' and Coaches' Joint Kick-Off Breakfast.
- Identify a space in your building to house your instructional coach 1 to 2 days per week. Have this space move-in ready by _____ (suggest teacher's desk or table, chair, electrical outlets, and trash can).
- Prepare a list of maven teachers for your instructional coach to observe during his/her first week in your school. (High school principals should identify all department chairpersons as well.) Inform these maven teachers of the coach's upcoming visit and tell them why they were selected.
- Be available to meet with the coach facilitator and your instructional coach in a brief (10 minutes or less) meeting structured around the following questions:
  - If you went into a classroom, what would you see that would help you *predict* that the kids will be successful?
  - What district initiatives are most widely implemented in your school? (List your district initiatives here.)
  - In general, what should the focus of classroom visits and professional conversations between your instructional coach and your teachers be? (List some suggestions that are relevant to your district here.)
  - How can your instructional coach best assist your school in achieving your school-improvement goals?
- Welcome and introduce your instructional coach to your staff and encourage teachers to invite the coach to their classrooms.

Chapter 6 Resources

SAMPLE WELCOME LETTER TO NEWLY HIRED COACHES

This letter can be used to welcome newly hired coaches to your district.

Date:

Dear Coaches:

We are excited to welcome new _____ coaches to our team as we begin year two of our coaching initiative! Our new coaches are: _____. The strengths and experiences these men and women will share with their colleagues are sure to have a far-reaching effect on teacher collegiality and student achievement in the area of _____.

Please review the schedule of meetings below. Do not hesitate to contact either of us if you have any questions or concerns regarding our fall plans.

Orientation Meetings Prior to _____ School Year:
>   *(Insert your plans here.)*

Coach-Coordinator (SÍ C-C) Meeting Schedule:
>   *(Insert your plans here.)*

Friday Focus Meeting Schedule:
>   *(Insert your plans here.)*

Other districtwide learning opportunities:
>   *(Insert your plans here.)*

As you can see, we will hit the ground running even before the official start of school. This year promises to be another exciting adventure as we work together to build collaborative coaching cultures in our schools. We both look forward to working with each of you.

Enjoy the next few weeks!

Your Coaching Champions

Chapter 8 Resources

All of the following activities are useful in ongoing training for coaches.

SAMPLE CULTURE OF COACHING ACTIVITY

Group Brainstorm

What does a school that has a fully developed culture of coaching look and sound like?

Group Brainstorm

What coaching activities best support the development of a culture of coaching in a school?

Independent Reflection

Review your past week's coaching activities, conversations, and roles. Write your response to the following essential question:

How can I take my activities, conversations, and roles and transform them into action that promotes a culture of coaching in the schools in which I serve?

SAMPLE GRIPES-TO-GOALS ACTIVITY

Directions: Working in groups of three, coaches will discuss the two questions below. Jot down your thoughts and ideas. Be prepared to share in large group.

Possible hindrances to full implementation of the coaching program:

_____

_____

_____

_____

_____

_____

_____

_____

Ways to break the chains that prevent full implementation of the coaching program:

_____

_____

_____

_____

_____

_____

_____

_____

Sample Peer Coaching Assignment

Mission Possible: Coach the Coach

Your mission, should you choose to accept it:

Draw a name from the "coaching hat" of another coach. (If you draw your close friend or your current coaching partner, put the name back and draw someone you know less well.)

During the next 4 weeks, schedule a time to coach a teacher at one of your schools—it can be a new person or someone you have worked with before. Have a preconference, videotaped 15- to 20-minute observation, and postconference with that person. (Tell the teacher this is for your growth more than his or hers!!)

Schedule your "Coach-Coach" to observe and videotape your pre- and postconferences. At the postconference, review the video with the teacher while your coach is videoing you watching the video with the teacher!! (Wheels in wheels).

Schedule your own postconference with your Coach-Coach. Let your coach practice coaching you in the postconference about the postconference.

Be prepared to share your coach-coaching experience with small groups during a Friday Focus (date to be announced).

Sample Coach—Coach Support

Guided Questions for Group Discussion

Give a brief overview of the purpose of your classroom observation and explain how you and the teacher arrived at that purpose.

What were the indicators from your postobservation conference that you achieved your purpose?

Sample Individual Reflection

Consulting My Own Compass

Based on the results of your peer coaching conversation, brainstorm a list for each category below:

My strengths as a coach:

_____

_____

_____

Opportunities for my growth:

_____

_____

_____

Action steps I need to take:

_____

_____

_____

My ahas:

_____

_____

_____

What I appreciate about the peer coaching experience:

_____

_____

_____

SAMPLE "CONSULTING THE COMPASS" ACTIVITY

Control   *Sphere of Influence*   *NoMB!*

Independent Reflection

Give each coach 10 index cards. Direct them to write one thing on each card that is currently causing them angst. Some people will use all 10 cards (and may want more!), while others may only need less than five. Participants may use as few as 1, but not more than 10 cards. Remember: One issue per card.

Leaders: You might want to play a recording of Patsy Cline's "Crazy" (1961) in the background while coaches are writing.

Leaders

When participants have finished writing on their index cards, leaders should initiate a discussion of those things that we, as individuals, can control, what falls into our sphere of influence, and what is really none of our business (NoMB!).

Following this discussion, have coaches sort their cards into three stacks: Control—Sphere of Influence—NoMB!

When they have finished sorting their cards, direct participants to do the following:

- Tear up all of the cards in you NoMB! stack.
- Place all of the cards in your Control stack in the *Let It Go!* box.
- Keep the cards in your Sphere of Influence stack and take time during the next week to discuss with your coaching partner or your facilitator ways you can transform these *crazies* into action that will promote a culture of coaching in the schools you serve.

SAMPLE IMAGINE ACTIVITY

Leaders: Occasionally, instructional coaches will encounter situations with teachers, supervisors, and fellow coaches that cause them to feel uncertain as to how to respond. Many times, such situations don't come with a single right answer, but they usually come with several acceptable ones. The Imagine Activity is designed to give your instructional coaches an opportunity to put themselves face to face with uncomfortable or even difficult situations and practice generating appropriate responses.

Introduction to the Activity: Play an excerpt from John Lennon's "Imagine" (1971) as you provide the background for this activity.

Directions: Cut apart the 10 different Imagine Scenarios. Divide your coaches into groups of two or three. Give each person in the group a different scenario. Each person in the group will read his or her scenario, and then the group will decide how to role play an appropriate response. Groups will need about 10 or 15 minutes to read their scenarios and plan their role play. Once groups have had time to read and prepare, ask volunteers to share with the large group.

To wrap up this activity, ask coaches to regroup to form pairs who will participate in a 3-minute standing conversation about how this activity will affect their responses to uncomfortable situations in the future.

Imagine. . . . Imagine. . . . Imagine. . . . Imagine. . . . Imagine. . . .

SAMPLE IMAGINE SCENARIOS

Imagine: A teacher, an administrator, or a central office person has made a decision with which you disagree. Someone comes to you, verbalizing an opinion similar to yours. What do you do to resist the temptation to engage in a gripe session? What are some examples of responses you could make that are professionally neutral? Why is remaining professionally neutral important—or is it?

Imagine: You have been asked by someone in your school to make a decision that has the potential for a more far-reaching impact that puts you slightly out of your comfort zone. How do you determine whether to make the decision on your own or to seek input from an administrator (principal, coach facilitator, coordinator, etc.)?

Imagine: You have just returned from one of the best professional learning events you've attended in a long time. You are eager to implement some of the new ideas you brought back to your schools. You want to make sure you have the approval you need to bring these ideas to life. What sorts of questions do you ask yourself to determine your first line of contact in the organizational chart in seeking that approval?

Imagine: A teacher comes to you and wants information that he mistakenly assumes you have. What kinds of questions do you ask yourself in deciding where to turn to get that information?

Imagine: You are entering a new social or professional situation. There are appearances, but there are also realities of which you may not be aware (norms, conflicts, histories, etc.). Realizing that you can't immediately discern these often subtle realities, how would you conduct your professional interactions with others in this setting?

Imagine: You and a group of colleagues are sharing a relaxing dinner at a local restaurant. All are talking and laughing, sharing stories about themselves and their families and friends. Suddenly, the conversation turns to school. Give specific examples of how you would put a fast end to the topic of school before someone has a chance to breach confidentiality in this casual, public setting.

Imagine: You and your buddy coach are sharing about your coaching experiences. How do you decide which coaching experiences are off-limits and which ones are not?

Imagine: You are in a staff meeting with your colleagues and supervisors. You notice that someone in the group is using body language that clearly communicates her disinterest and/or displeasure with the meeting—rolling eyes, whispering, e-mailing, texting, and so forth. You want to say something to your colleague about professionalism, but you're not sure what or how to say it. What might be the best way to handle this situation for all involved?

Imagine: As an instructional coach in at least two different schools, you have the opportunity to see and hear many things. Some things you see would make you proud as a peacock, but you have encountered a situation that makes you want to put your head in the sand. What kinds of things rise to the level that someone in higher authority needs to know about it?

To whom do you turn for guidance if you aren't sure?

Imagine: You have been asked by an administrator (principal, coaching facilitator, coordinator, director) to provide information about someone's job performance. What is your best coaching response?

Imagine. . . . Imagine. . . . Imagine. . . . Imagine. . . . Imagine. . . .

Sample Friday Focus

Date: _____

Use this form to communicate agenda items for our Friday meetings. Agenda items must be submitted to your coaching facilitator by noon on Thursday.

Celebrations:

_____

_____

_____

_____

_____

Concerns:*

_____

_____

_____

_____

_____

Requests:

_____

_____

_____

_____

_____

Worth Sharing:

_____

_____

_____

_____

_____

Questions:

_____

_____

_____

_____

*When presenting concerns, coaches are encouraged to have at least one suggested solution to present as well.

References

Achebe, C. (1992). *Things fall apart.* New York: Knopf.

AdvanceEd. (2010). Leveraging change for school improvement. Alpharetta, GA: Author. Retrieved from http://www.advanc-ed.org

Allen, D., & LeBlanc, A. (2005). *Collaborative peer coaching that improves instruction: The 2+2 performance appraisal model.* Thousand Oaks, CA: Corwin.

Barkley, S. G. (2010). *Quality teaching in a culture of coaching.* Lanham, MD: Rowman & Littlefield Education.

Barth, R. S. (2003). *Lessons learned: Shaping relationships and the culture of the workplace.* Thousand Oaks, CA: Corwin.

Barth, R. (2006). Improving relationships within the school house. *Educational Leadership, 63*(6), 8–13.

Bean, R., & Isler, W. (2008, July 28). The school board wants to know: Why literacy coaching? *Literacy Coaching Clearinghouse,* pp. 1–3.

Brozo, W., & Fisher, D. (2010). Literacy starts with the teachers. *Educational Leadership, 67*(6), 74–77.

The Center for Comprehensive School Reform and Improvement. (2007). *Principal as instructional leader: Designing a coaching program that fits* (Issue brief). Washington, DC: Learning Point Associates.

Childress, H. (1998). Seventeen reasons why football is better than high school. *The Phi Delta Kappan, 79*(8), 616–619.

Clary, D., Oglan, V., & Styslinger, M. (2008). It is not just about content: preparing content area teachers to be literacy leaders. *Literacy Coaching Clearinghouse* (September 15), 1–5.

Collins, J. C. (2001). *Good to great: Why some companies make the leap—and others don't.* New York: Harper Business.

Costa, A., & Garmston, R. (2002). *Cognitive coaching: A foundation for renaissance schools.* Norwood, MA: Christopher-Gordon.

Covey, S. R. (1989). *Seven habits of highly effective people: Powerful lessons in personal change.* New York: Fireside Books.

Darling-Hammond, L. (2005). Teaching as a profession: Lessons in teacher preparation and professional development. *The Phi Delta Kappan, 87*(3), 237–240.

Darling-Hammond, L. (2010–11, Winter). Soaring systems: High flyers all have equitable funding, shared curriculum, quality teaching. *American Educator,* p. 22.

Darling-Hammond, L., & Richardson, N. (2009). Teacher learning: What matters? *How Teachers Learn, 66*(5), 46–53.

Darling-Hammond, L., Wei, R., Andree, A., Richardson, N., & Orphanos, S. (2009). The state of the profession: Study measures status of professional development. *Journal of Staff Development, 30*(2), 42–44, 46–50.

Davis, B. (2008). *How to coach teachers who don't think like you: Using literacy strategies to coach across content areas.* Thousand Oaks, CA: Corwin.

de Saint-Exupery, A. (n.d.). Antoine de Saint-Exupery quotes. Retrieved from http://www.finestquotes.com/author_quotes-author-Antoine%20 de%20Saint-Exupery-page-0.htm

DePorter, B. (n.d.). *The impact of quantum learning.* Baltimore, MD: Johns Hopkins University College of Education New Horizons for Learning. Retrieved from http://www.newhorizons.org/strategies/accelerated/ deporter2.htm

Drucker, P. F., Collins, J. C., Kotler, P., Kouzes, J., Rodin, J., Rangan, V. K., & Hesselbein, F. (2008). *The five most important questions you will ever ask about your organization.* New York: Leader to Leader Institute.

Friedman, T. L. (2005). *The world is flat: a brief history of the twenty-first century.* New York: Farrar, Straus and Giroux.

Fullan, M. (2001). *Leading in a culture of change.* San Francisco: Jossey-Bass.

Fullan, M. (2008). *The six secrets of change: What the best leaders do to help their organizations survive and thrive.* San Francisco: Jossey-Bass.

Fullan, M. (2010). *All systems go: The change imperative for whole system reform.* Thousand Oaks, CA: Corwin.

Gardner, H. (2006). *Changing minds: The art and science of changing our own and other people's minds.* Boston: Harvard Business School Press.

Gladwell, M. (2002). *The tipping point: How little things can make a big difference.* Boston: Back Bay Books.

Gladwell, M. (2008). *Outliers: The story of success.* New York: Little, Brown.

Guskey, T. (2000). *Evaluating professional development.* Thousand Oaks, CA: Corwin.

Guskey, T., & Yoon, K. (2009). What works in professional development? *The Phi Delta Kappan, 90*(7), 495–500.

Heath, C., & Heath, D. (2010). *Switch: How to change things when change is hard.* New York: Broadway Books.

Heath, D., & Heath, C. (2007). *Made to stick: Why some ideas survive and others die.* New York: Random House.

Hollingshead, A. B. (2000). Perceptions of expertise and transactive memory in work relationships. *Group Processes & Intergroup Relations, 3*(3), 257–267. doi: 10.1177/1368430200033002.

Holmes, O. (2001). *The autocrat at the breakfast table.* Boston: Indypublish.com

Killion, J. (2007). Web of support strengthens the effectiveness of school-based coaches. *Journal of Staff Development, 28*(1), 10–12, 14–16, 18.

Killion, J. (2009). Coaches' roles, responsibilities, and reach. In J. Knight (Ed.), *Coaching approaches & perspectives* (pp. 7–28). Thousand Oaks, CA: Corwin.

Killion, J., & Harrison, C. (2006). *Taking the lead: New roles for teachers and school-based coaches.* Oxford, OH: NSDC.

Kise, J. A. G. (2006). *Differentiated coaching: A framework for helping teachers change.* Thousand Oaks, CA: Corwin.

Knight, J. (2004). Instructional coaching. *StrateNotes: University of Kansas Center for Instructional Coaching, 13*(3) 1–5. Retrieved from http://www.instructional-coach.org/images/downloads/articles/nov_stratenotes.pdf

Knight, J. (2005). A primer on instructional coaches. *Principal Leadership, 5*(9), 16–21.

Knight, J. (2007). *Instructional coaching: A partnership approach to improving instruction.* Thousand Oaks, CA: Corwin.

Knight, J. (Ed.). (2009). *Coaching approaches & perspectives.* Thousand Oaks, CA: Corwin.

Knight, J. (2011). *Unmistakable impact: A partnership approach for dramatically improving instruction.* Thousand Oaks, CA: Corwin.

Kowal, J., & Steiner, L. (2007, September). *Issue brief—instructional coaching.* Washington, DC: Center for Comprehensive School Reform and Improvement.

Lambert, L. (2003). *Leadership capacity for lasting school improvement.* Alexandria, VA: ASCD.

The last 1000 years. (1999). Bath, UK: Paragon.

Learning Forward. (2011). *Evidence of effectiveness.* Oxford, OH: Author. http://www.learningforward.org/standfor/definition.cfm

Mangin, M. (2009, January 24). To have or not to have? Factors that influence district decisions about literacy coaches. *Literacy Coaching Clearinghouse*, 1–3.

Manguel, A., & Guadalupi, G. (2000). *The dictionary of imaginary places.* New York: Harcourt Brace.

Maxwell, J. C. (2001). *The 21 irrefutable laws of leadership workbook.* Nashville, TN: Thomas Nelson.

McEwan-Adkins, E. K. (2009). *10 traits of highly effective schools: Raising the achievement bar for all students.* Thousand Oaks, CA: Corwin.

Morse, A. (2009). *Cultivating a math coaching practice: A guide for K–8 math educators.* Thousand Oaks, CA: Corwin.

Moxley, D., & Taylor, R. (2006). *Literacy coaching: A handbook for school leaders.* Thousand Oaks, CA: Corwin.

Neufeld, B., & Roper, D. (2003). *Coaching: A strategy for developing instructional capacity. Promises & practicalities.* The Aspen Institute Aspen Program on Education. Washington, DC: The Annenberg Institute for School Reform.

Oczukus, L. (2009). *Interactive think-aloud lessons.* New York: Scholastic.

Patterson, K., Grenny, J., Maxfield, D., McMillan, R., & Switzler, A. (2008). *Influencer: The power to change anything.* New York: McGraw-Hill.

Pavelka, P. (2009). *Differentiating instruction in a whole-group setting.* East Lyme, CT: Husky Trail Press.

Petti, A. D. (2010). Circles of leadership. *Journal of Staff Development, 31*(6), 52–54, 56.

Pink, D. (2005). *A whole new mind: Why right-brainers will rule the future.* New York: Berkley Publishing Group.

Pink, D. (2009). *Drive: The surprising truth about what motivates us.* New York: Riverhead Books.

Reeves, D. B. (2009). *Leading change in your school: How to conquer myths, build commitment, and get results*. Alexandria, VA: Association for Supervision and Curriculum Development.

Reiss, K. (2009). Leadership coaching. In J. Knight (Ed.), *Coaching approaches & perspectives* (pp. 166–191). Thousand Oaks, CA: Corwin.

Sadder, M., & Nidus, G. (2009). *The literacy coach's game plan: Making teacher collaboration, student learning, and school improvement a reality*. Newark, DE: International Reading Association.

Saphier, J., & West, L. (2009/2010). How coaches can maximize student learning. *The Phi Delta Kappan, 91*(4), 46–50.

St. Peter, A. (2010). *The greatest quotations of all time*. Bloomington, IN: Xlibris.

Schmoker, M. (2011). *Focus: Elevating the essentials to radically improve student learning*. Alexandria, VA: ASCD.

Schmoker, M. J. (2006). *Results now*. Alexandria, VA: ASCD.

Scott, S. (2004). *Fierce conversations: Achieving success at work & in life, one conversation at a time*. New York: Berkley Books.

Thoreau, H. (2011). *Walden*. Macon, GA: Mercer University Press.

Tschannen-Moran, B., & Tschannen-Moran, M. (2010). *Evocative coaching: Transforming schools one conversation at a time*. San Francisco: Jossey-Bass.

Tschannen-Moran, M., & Tschannen-Moran, B. (2011). Taking a strengths-based focus improves school climate. *Journal of School Leadership, 21*(3), 422–448.

United States Department of Education. (2009, April 24). Doing what works. Retrieved from http://www2.ed.gov

Vanderburg, M., & Stephens, D. (2009, January 2). What teachers say they changed because of their coach and how they think their coach helped them. *Literacy Coaching Clearinghouse*, 1–4.

Vygotsky, L. S. (1978). *Thought and language*. Cambridge, MA: MIT Press.

Wheatley, M. J., & Kellner-Rogers, M. (1999a). *A simpler way*. San Francisco, CA: Berrett-Koehler.

Wheatley, M. J., & Kellner-Rogers, M. (1999b, June). What do we measure and why? Questions about the uses of measurement. *Journal for Strategic Performance Measurement*. Retrieved from http://www.margaretwheatley.com/articles/whymeasure.html

Wilson, P. (n.d.). Blob tree. Wimpy player. Retrieved from http://www.youthblog.org/2005/08/pip-wilsons-blob-tree.html

Facilitator's Guide to *How to Build an Instructional Coaching Program for Maximum Capacity*

For Use with Study Groups or Professional Learning Communities

The purpose of this facilitator's guide is to assist the reader in preparing to lead a professional development series or to facilitate a professional learning community (PLC) focused study, allowing facilitators to actively engage participants in interesting yet easy-to-implement learning opportunities.

Each chapter guide begins with *The Music* and *The Metaphor*. We learned from Quantum Learning© the importance of incorporating music and metaphors into our teaching to promote interest, connections, and long-term memory and retention. The music and metaphors we have chosen are simply suggestions. The facilitator is free to substitute music and metaphors that best suit each unique audience. You may choose to have the music playing in the background as participants enter and use it to segue to your first activity, or you may incorporate the music into a particular activity. In addition, we have attempted to provide ample activities to use with each chapter and set no expectation that all activities must be completed or that they can only be completed in the order in which we present them here. The facilitator is encouraged to select the activities in each chapter that are most appropriate for the groups, schedules, and locations with which you will work.

Chapter 1 *Prevailing Winds: Navigating the Perfect Storm*

The Music   "Blowin' in the Wind" by Bob Dylan (1962)

The Metaphor   Prevailing winds are powerful and affect the climate
                   of a geographical area. Other winds may blow this
                   way and that, but the prevailing winds are the ones
                   you can count on over the long haul. The current
                   research on educational reform affects the climate of
                   classrooms, schools, and school districts, but politi-
                   cal wind blow strongly, too. Savvy leaders pay
                   attention to the prevailing conditions as they make
                   decisions and prepare for unexpected storms.

Suggested Activities

1. Ask participants to listen to an excerpt of Bob Dylan's
   "Blowin' in the Wind" (1962). After listening, have them jot
   down images that came to mind as they heard the song.
   Allow time for participants to *Turn to Your Neighbor* and share
   with an elbow partner.

2. Read aloud the metaphor for Chapter 1. Invite discussion
   about the changes that your school or district is experiencing.
   How are teachers and administrators in your district responding to these changes—what feelings are evoked by the
   changes?

3. Introduce the topic of implementing an instructional coaching
   program as a change initiative. Quickly survey the group to
   determine individual and collective knowledge and experience with instructional coaching and with leading change.

4. Depending on the size of the group, distribute one or two
   brief articles about instructional coaching and leading change.
   Divide the group into two groups (or four, if you have a large
   group). Give one group a copy of the instructional coaching
   article and one group a copy of the leading change article. Tell
   each group they will have several minutes to silently read
   their article. As they read, they should underline important
   facts, put a question mark (?) next to things that are unclear,

place an exclamation mark (!) next to ideas with which they agree, draw an "X" next to statements with which they disagree, and put a star (*) beside "ahas" they discover. When they finish reading, each group should discuss the article in light of their markings and identify one person from the group to summarize in the large group. (This activity may be modified and used as an outside assignment if your group meets on a regular basis.)

Suggested resources for this activity include:

Heath, C., & Heath, D. (2011). Overcoming resistance to change. *School Administrator, 3*, 28–32.

Killion, J. (2008). Courage, confidence, clarity mark the pathway to change. *Journal of Staff Development, 29*(4), 55–59.

Knight, J. (2005). A primer on instructional coaches. *Principal Leadership, 5*(9), 16–21.

Knight, J. (2007). Five key points to building a coaching program. *Journal of Staff Development, 28*(1), 26–31.

---

5. If your group meets on a regular basis, select one of the books below and facilitate a book study. Or, you might choose to select a book and assign each participant or pairs of participants to read a different chapter and make a presentation to the group.

Fullan, M. (2008). *The six secrets of change: What the best leaders do to help their organizations survive and thrive.* San Francisco: Jossey-Bass.

Fullan, M. (2010). *Motion leadership: The skinny on becoming change savvy.* Thousand Oaks, CA: Corwin.

Knight, J. (2011). *Unmistakable impact: A partnership approach for dramatically improving instruction.* Thousand Oaks, CA: Corwin.

Senge, P. M. (2006). *The fifth discipline: The art and practice of the learning organization.* New York: Doubleday/Currency.

---

6. The authors identify five rational reasons for implementing an instructional coaching program in your school or district:

a. Student achievement is the goal.

b. Research shows that more effective teachers lead to greater student achievement.

   c. Research shows that skilled teacher-centered instructional coaching leads to more effective teaching.

   d. Research shows that coaching leads to far greater implementation of strategies learned in professional development.

   e. Research shows that teachers reap many additional professional benefits from coaching.

Write the five rational reasons for implementing an instructional coaching program in large letters on separate pieces of chart paper. Divide the group into five smaller groups (or fewer, if your group is small). Give each group one of the rational reasons chart papers. Ask each group to list the coaching connections to their rational reason. In other words, how does instructional coaching connect to improving student achievement? List some ideas. After each group has had a few minutes to generate and write their ideas, post the charts around the room. Ask participants to conduct a gallery walk around the room, adding one new idea to each chart. Review the lists and summarize the activity.

7. The authors point out some of the emotional benefits of coaching and emphasize the importance of helping teachers embrace coaching on an emotional level. Discuss the importance of making an emotional connection in regard to coaching. What are the benefits? Are there any drawbacks? If so, what are they?

In business, students are taught to create an "elevator pitch"—a way to sell yourself or your product in the time it takes to go up in an elevator with someone. In this activity, groups, pairs or individuals may use the material in the chapter or additional resources to create a brief pitch for instructional coaching in your school or district. Teams may demonstrate their pitch through role-play in front of the group.

To organize our thoughts while writing this book, the authors chose a metaphor of a sea voyage. Develop your own metaphor to describe your experience with implementing an instructional coaching initiative so far. First, list the salient characteristics of your experience. Then, identify another experience that has similar characteristics. Describe your metaphor in words or in pictures.

Salient characteristics/traits	Other experiences that share these traits

My Metaphor for Implementing Instructional Coaching:

Chapter 2 *Dead Reckoning: Beginning With the End in Mind*

The Music: "Simplify" by Gary Hoey (2010)

The Metaphor: In *Walden,* Henry David Thoreau (2011) writes,

> In the midst of this chopping sea of civilized life, such are the clouds and storms and quicksands and thousand-and-one items to be allowed for, that a man has to live, if he would not founder and go to the bottom and not make his port at all, by dead reckoning, and he must be a great calculator indeed who succeeds. Simplify, simplify. (p. 89)

Suggested Activities

1. Letting go of certainty can be a daunting yet necessary step in the change process, as the authors discuss in Chapter 2. Ask participants to reflect on a time in their lives when they let go of certainty. One or two volunteers may share their stories

with the large group. Probing questions might include: (a) Was there a single, memorable moment that served as the impetus for letting go? If so, can you tell us about it? (b) Once you let go, what kept you moving toward the change? (c) What advice would you give to our group as we work toward facilitating a change initiative in our organization?

2. The authors state that "dead reckoning is not dead certainty" (page 14). Discuss this statement with an "elbow partner."

3. Post your school's or district's vision statement for everyone in the group to view. Engage participants in a round table discussion of what the vision means to them, their assessment of how "on track" your organization is in moving toward your vision, any evidence they have to support their perceptions, and what changes they believe need to occur to either refine or rewrite your vision statement (or what changes they believe need to occur to get the organization back on track to moving toward your vision).

4. Distribute copies of the illustration from page 16 (concentric circles of vision *that all share the same center*). Discuss the illustration using your district vision, school vision, and your vision for coaching. Emphasize the point that the coaching vision is embedded in the district's vision in this illustration. Determine whether your coaching vision is embedded in your district's broader vision.

5. Discuss the following questions about professional development in your district. Be sure to ask for specific evidence to support the group's responses:

   a. Does our current professional development model encourage and foster the use of professional learning communities?

   b. Does our current professional development model support adult learning and collaboration by providing our teachers and administrators the knowledge and skills needed to collaborate?

   c. Is our current professional development model designed to incorporate a variety of adult learning strategies?

   d. Does our current professional development model include *job-embedded* learning opportunities?

   e. Most importantly, does our current professional development model support and align with our student achievement goals?

6. Refer to the opening metaphor for this chapter. Thoreau tells us to "simplify, simplify." Amazingly, to live the simple life, you must live the carefully navigated life. A school or district is no different. Discuss the connection between a simple plan and a detailed, thorough plan.

7. In the Middle Ages, knights fought for their honor in a field (*campus*, in Latin) so they came to be called *campions* or fighters in the field. The term has evolved to *champion* and is often used to refer to a winner of a contest. A champion can also mean a person who is an advocate for an idea or cause. Why might coaching need a "fighter in the field" in your school or district? What kind of person would make a good champion for coaching?

8. Brainstorm a list of coaching champions in your district who should be part of your planning team. Does your list include stakeholders from the district, school, and classroom levels? What role will each member play in the planning process?

9. Use the following questions from the administrative model discussed in this chapter:
   a. What are the specific goals of your coaching program?
   b. What is the role of a coach in your program?
   c. Will the coaches work for one school or for the district? If the district, how many schools will they serve?
   d. Who will supervise the coaches and who will participate in hiring?
   e. How will the coaches be matched with schools?
   f. Who will champion the coaches?
   g. What rules and regulations will affect the hiring, placement, evaluation, and tenure of coaches?
   h. How will district–coach and principal–coach communication occur?
   i. With whom will the coaches work within the school?
   j. How long will the coaches serve in their positions?
   k. What are the district policies and parameters for coaches?

10. The authors identify some potential "squalls" or problems that may arise as you begin to implement your coaching program. What potential squalls might you anticipate in your district? What plans can you make now to avert these squalls?

Chapter 3 *Sounding the Depths: Using Data for Reflecting, Refining, and Celebrating*

The Music: "The Wreck of the *Edmund Fitzgerald*" by Gordon Lightfoot (1976)

The Metaphor: The *Edmund Fitzgerald* sank in Lake Superior in 1975, but famous shipwrecks such as that one have been the subjects of ballads for centuries. In 1707, in what is considered to be one of the greatest naval disasters of all time, more than 1,400 sailors perished at the British Isles of Scilly, off the coast of Cornwall. Four ships of the British Fleet were lost, and although no one knows the exact death toll, bodies, personal effects, and the wreckage of the ships were washing up on the shore for days. It is believed that the sailors' inability to correctly calculate their longitude—and thus know their position in relation to the rocks of Scilly—was the reason the fleet went off course and wrecked. Sailors realized their old methods of "dead reckoning" (calculating your position based on a previously determined position; see Chapter 2) were inadequate, and the search began for an alternative navigational tool. British Parliament passed the Longitude Act of 1714, which offered a large cash prize for anyone who could invent a device that would assist in calculating a ship's position. After many years and much trial and error, marine chronometers were finally invented that allowed sailors to calculate time while on ship. With this precise knowledge, mariners could calculate longitude and make an accurate reading of their current location.

Suggested Activities

1. Listen to Gordon Lightfoot's recording of "The Wreck of the *Edmund Fitzgerald*" (1976). Tell the story of the invention of marine chronometers. Generate a lighthearted discussion around any "shipwrecks" the group is familiar with in an educational setting. Ask, "What do we use for a chronometer in our work?"

2. Communicate the need for a navigation plan for your program. Based on an assignment developed by Susan Scott in her book, *Fierce Conversations*, write and practice a 30-second *stump speech* that explains "where we are going, why we are going there; who is going with us and how we will get there" (Scott, 2004, p. 81).

3. We learned from Killion and Harrison (2006) that expectations of any coaching program are at least twofold: We "expect to see increased academic performance and improved professional collaboration" (p. 141). Ask the group to identify the types of information you will need to assess whether you have met or exceeded your instructional coaching program goals.

4. Refer to your response to Activity 2. As you consider the different types of information you will need to measure success, identify the purpose of each.

5. Sort the results of Activity 3 into the following categories: Data to Evaluate the Coaching Program, Data to Evaluate Leaders of the Coaching Program, Data to Evaluate Coaches, Data to Monitor the Effectiveness of Individual Teacher–Coach Relationships. Discuss the following questions: What purposes are most important for your data-collection and -assessment plan? Which do you think will be the most difficult to achieve? How frequently will you need feedback in order to evaluate the program, the leaders, and the coaches?

6. Distribute copies of the data-collection forms included in the **Chapter 3 Resources** section of the book. Ask participants to examine the sample forms in light of their conclusions in Activities 2 through 4. How can any of the forms be adapted for use in your organization?

7. The authors refer to Killion's (2009) description of *coaching shallow* and *coaching deep*. What might each of these types of coaching look like in your organization? Are there times when *coaching shallow* is warranted? How will you and your coaches know it is time to move to "deep water'?

8. Provide a brief background on the 1960s television show *Sea Hunt* (Buxbaum, 1958–1961) and then play an excerpt of one of the shows you download from YouTube (www.youtube.com). Using the "turn to your neighbor" strategy, ask participants to discuss with a partner the "treasures" and other

"hidden things" that coaching might uncover in your organization? How will you leverage your findings for whole school or district improvement?

9. Display a poster-size copy or make individual copies of Pip Wilson's *Blob Tree* (n.d.), which you can purchase and download from www.pipwilson.com. If using a single poster, distribute sticky dots to participants and ask them to place their sticker on the blob tree to indicate where they are in their understanding of the process of building an instructional coaching program or in their understanding of their role in the coaching program. Allow time for all participants to explain why they identify with those particular "blobs." If using individual copies of the tree, participants can circle the blobs with which they identify.

10. Brainstorm a list of things that are worth learning and need to be celebrated in your school or district. Every day for one week, celebrate in small ways something worth learning. Reflect on any changes you might see during this experiment and plan to report to the group.

11. Review the *Steps to a Coaching Program Assessment Plan* on page 47. As a group, assess your progress in accomplishing each step of the assessment-planning process. Discuss any refinements you may want to make and develop an action plan and timeline for making changes.

Chapter 4 *Ready, Set, Sail: Selecting the Coaching Crew*

The Music: "Son of a Son of a Sailor" by Jimmy Buffett (1978)

The Metaphor: Before the Seaman's Act of 1915, many sailors were "shanghaied" or conscripted to join the crew of a ship. "Boarding masters" were men who were paid by the body for merchant ship crews and frequently they resorted to tactics such as drugging and kidnapping men and forging their names to the ships' articles. A man would wake up and find himself on a 9- to 12-month voyage! While some coaches (and administrators) may feel that this has happened to them when they find themselves awakened by ever-increasing responsibilities, conscription is no way to staff a school. When the school system "fleet" sets sail on a new school year, all the crew must be willing and ready for the challenge, but the coach, who is the model teacher, must be the right crewman for that vessel and that voyage. To modify a metaphor from the bestselling book *Good to Great* (Collins, 2001), the captain must get the wrong people off the ship, get the right people on the ship, and get everyone in the right places on the ship. This must be done intentionally and thoughtfully before you can even decide the path of the ship.

Suggested Activities

1. Review several of the decisions you made earlier regarding the coach selection process:
   - The goals of your coaching program
   - The role of a coach in your coaching program
   - The number of schools each coach will serve
   - The coaching supervisor
   - The hiring committee
   - Matching the coaches to the schools they will serve
   - The coaching champion(s)
   - Policy and rules for hiring, placement, and evaluation of coaches

   Discuss the following questions: In what ways might your particular coaching goals impact the characteristics of the person(s) you hire for the job? Based on the decisions you have made so far, who should participate in the coach search/interview team? What are some ways the selection team can come to consensus on the roles and qualities of an instructional coach in our program?

2. Using your Coaching Administrative Model, create a 5- to 10-sentence paragraph describing your coaching program that you can use as a promotional literature piece.

3. Create a concept map of the perfect coach. In the center of the page, write the word *coach*, with the qualities discussed in the chapter all around. Think of other attributes of a great coach and add them to the map.

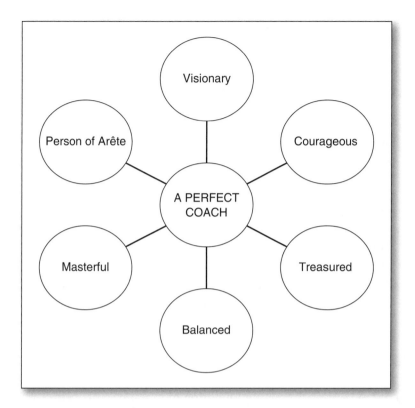

4. Examine the imperative qualities of coaches outlined below and try to reach consensus about what each looks like and sounds like to you and your organization's setting:

A quality coach is . . .

- visionary
- courageous
- a masterful teacher
- balanced
- treasured
- a person of arête

Create a "looks like/sounds like" chart similar to the one below for each of the IQCs.

Visionary	
Looks like	*Sounds like*

5. Discuss the suggested questions for each imperative coaching quality outlined in Chapter 4 to determine which ones will be most applicable to your interview process. Generate your own questions for discovering the imperative qualities you seek in an instructional coach.

Some questions that might reveal a visionary include the following:

- Describe the mission and vision of your current school or district. How do you see your role in living out that mission in the organization?
- Share your vision of the future of education.
- How do your own personal values affect your role as a teacher leader?
- Describe one of your most meaningful professional development experiences. How did it impact your practice? Why?

Some questions that might reveal workplace courage include the following:

- Describe a time when you were given a large and complex task to complete. How did you tackle it?
- Describe the best supervisor you have had. What made him or her stand out from among the rest?
- What kinds of management styles or techniques do you find empowering and exciting?
- If you were given a large job with a short amount of time to complete it, would you prefer to work with a team or on your own? Why?
- Have you been given a task and told to work with a group of adults who did not want to work with you? If so, what did you do to make sure the task was completed?

Some questions that might reveal a masterful teacher include the following:

- Describe a recent lesson you have taught. What were the students doing? What would you wish to improve next time?
- Pretend I walked into your classroom unannounced on a Wednesday morning. What might I see? There are many different instructional models, from direct instruction to problem-based or inquiry learning. What are some different models you have used successfully in the classroom?
- What do you do in your classroom to make sure you meet the needs of diverse learners?

- If we asked you to teach a lesson on _____ to a group of students you did not know, what would you do to prepare? How would you approach the lesson?

Some questions that might reveal balance include the following:

- We all have challenges in balancing work and personal responsibilities. What are some ways you have handled these challenges in the past?
- What are some ways that you use your personal experiences to enrich your professional life?
- Coaching requires unpredictable hours and occasional travel. Can you envision yourself making the adjustment to a schedule that does not always conform to the school-year calendar?
- Teaching and coaching require a lot of time-management skills. What methods do you use to keep on top of all the tasks that you must complete in your current job?
- Describe a time when you have been under extreme professional or personal stress. What strategies did you use to respond to this challenge?

Some questions that might reveal treasures include the following:

- What do you think your most important contributions to your current school or district have been?
- How would your current principal or supervisor describe you?
- How would your colleagues describe you?
- What would be the most difficult thing about leaving your current job?
- What kind of contribution do you think you can make to our school or district?

Some reference questions that might reveal this include the following:

- When you were supervising (coach applicant's name), how would you describe your day-to-day working relationship?
- If (coach applicant's name) decides to take another position, what will you or your organization miss the most?

Some questions that might reveal arête include the following:

- Tell me about something in which you believe passionately.
- If you could change anything about education today, what would it be?

- Describe your greatest strength and your greatest weakness.
- If a student tells you about a serious problem he is having with another teacher, how would you handle it? Would you handle it differently if a colleague came to you with such a problem?
- Think of the biggest professional challenge you have experienced. How did you handle it? Would you handle it differently if you had it to do over?

6. View a short clip from the film *Amazing Grace* (2007). It is the story of William Wilberforce, a leader in the abolition of the slave trade. Wilberforce reshaped the political and moral attitudes of the 18th century. In addition to his tireless political work, he was generous with his time and money and known for his warmth and hospitality. Although Wilberforce became an outspoken proponent of the abolition of slavery, he did not take himself too seriously. His nature remained unchanged—he "remained outwardly cheerful, interested, and respectful, tactfully urging others towards his new faith" (Hague, 2007, pp. 99–102). Think of a historical or fictional character that is meaningful to you and who embodies the imperative qualities of coaches. Outline the person's character traits and relate them to traits you will look for in a coach.

7. Read the poem *If* by Rudyard Kipling (1996). Assign one section to each member of your group. Identify how the qualities described in each section are important to a coach and create an interview or written-response question that might help you determine if an applicant might have that quality.

If

If you can keep your head when all about you

Are losing theirs and blaming it on you;

If you can trust yourself when all men doubt you

But make allowance for their doubting too:

If you can wait and not be tired by waiting,

Or being lied about, don't deal in lies,

Or being hated don't give way to hating,

And yet don't look too good, nor talk too wise;

If you can dream—and not make dreams your master;

If you can think—and not make thoughts your aim,

If you can meet with Triumph and Disaster

And treat those two imposters just the same:

If you can bear to hear the truth you've spoken

Twisted by knaves to make a trap for fools,

Or watch the things you gave your life to, broken,

And stoop and build 'em up with worn-out tools;

If you can make one heap of all your winnings

And risk it on one turn of pitch-and-toss,

And lose, and start again at your beginnings

And never breathe a word about your loss:

If you can force your heart and nerve and sinew

To serve your turn long after they are gone,

And so hold on when there is nothing in you

Except the Will which says to them: "Hold on!"

If you can talk with crowds and keep your virtue,

Or walk with Kings—nor lose the common touch,

If neither foes nor loving friends can hurt you,

If all men count with you, but none too much:

If you can fill the unforgiving minute

With sixty seconds' worth of distance run,

Yours is the Earth and everything that's in it,

And—which is more—you'll be a Man, my son!

—Rudyard Kipling (1996, pp. 96–97)

Chapter 5 *O, Captain, My Captain: Preparing the Principal*

The Music: "The Union" by Louis Gottschalk (1862)

The Metaphor: *O Captain! My Captain!*, the famous Walt Whitman poem (1865), was penned in tribute to the 16th president of the United States, Abraham Lincoln, and published following Lincoln's assassination: "O Captain! my Captain! our fearful trip is done; The ship has weather'd every rack, the prize we sought is won . . . " Even in the face of his leader's death, the poet's voice cries out to him, vulnerably exposing his need for his captain to rise up and witness their sail into the victor's port. Whitman's pleas not only underscore his unyielding reliance upon his leader, his captain; his impassioned pleas also underscore his unfaltering desire to share the victory celebration with his captain. In education, we, too, depend on strong and vital leaders—leaders who are equipped, prepared, and fully present in major and minor milestones and ultimate victories.

Suggested Activities

1. Play an excerpt from "Union" by Gottschalk (1862) and relate the following background information: In a 2009 interview on NPR's *Morning Edition*, musical commentator Miles Hoffman offered his answer to the question, "If Abraham Lincoln had an iPod, what music would he have chosen to put on it?" One of the compositions Hoffman identified was Gottschalk's "Union" (1862). A Southern-born piano virtuoso and composer from Louisiana, Gottschalk wove several familiar tunes, including "The Star Spangled Banner," "Yankee Doodle," and "Hail Columbia," into this well-received, patriotic medley (www .gottschalk.fr/Biographie/Biographie-eng.htm). Regardless of his Southern heritage, Gottschalk was a supporter of the Union cause—a worthy cause—led by a man whom Gottschalk respected, admired, and honored. As highlighted in Chapter 5, "People don't at first follow worthy causes. They follow worthy leaders who promote worthwhile causes" (Maxwell, 2001, p. 155). A well-constructed principal-preparation plan will enable

worthy principal leaders to successfully implement your district's instructional coaching initiative. With your group, discuss ways to assist the worthy principal leaders in your district as they promote and support your coaching initiative.

2. The authors recommend seven topics to address in principal-preparation plans. Review these seven topics and generate a series of questions you want to have answered before proceeding with your planning for principal preparation.

- Leading a change initiative
- How instructional coaching supports and facilitates change
- The role of the instructional coach
- The role of the principal
- The role of the coaching champion
- Communication among stakeholders
- The principal–coach memorandum of understanding (MOU)

3. Identify other pertinent topics for principal preparation your district deems necessary.

4. Discuss other change initiatives your district has experienced. What aspects of these earlier initiatives were successful? What decisions supported their success? What aspects of the change were less successful? What could have made the change better, easier, more successful, and so forth?

5. Brainstorm a list of potential experts on leading change you could enlist to assist in your principal-preparation plans. Identify the various roles they could assume (presenter, site-based consultant, etc.). Think about how much time you should devote to this particular topic. Consider the benefits of surveying principals and other administrators in your district to determine experience and attitudes regarding implementing major change initiatives.

6. Using the "A Coach Is . . . A Coach Is Not" activity from Killion and Harrison's work, *Taking the Lead* (2006), identify qualities participants believe fit each column. Discuss reasons for assigning qualities to one side of the T-chart or the other.

7. Many principals and district leaders engage in "learning walks" to observe and take note of the types and quality of teaching and learning behaviors occurring in their schools.

Consider the idea of teamed learning walks in which participants conduct walks in pairs for the purpose of identifying stellar classrooms—those classrooms in which students appear to be highly focused and actively engaged in learning. Upon completion of the learning walk, pairs engage in a discussion about the classrooms they identified with regard to the *specific teacher and student behaviors they observed* in these classrooms that led them to their conclusions. (Note: The purpose of this activity is not to rank teachers but to reach consensus on what exceptional teaching and learning strategies look and sound like.) Identified teacher and student behaviors from all of the walks can then be compiled into a list of stellar strategies. This list may be used to assist principals in determining a focus for coaching activities in their schools.

8. Barkley (2010) identifies four communication models used in the coaching process:

- A *two-way model* between the principal and teacher and between the coach and teacher, but not between the principal and the coach
- A *silent mentor model* in which the principal and teacher talk to each other, the teacher and coach talk to each other, and the principal talks to the coach without expectation of feedback from the instructional coach
- The *positive reinforcement model* in which two-way communication exists between the teacher and coach and between the teacher and principal, but only positive information is communicated from the coach to the principal
- A *full communication model* in which the principal, teacher, and instructional coach all communicate with each other, regardless of the positive or negative nature of the communication

Discuss the pros and cons of using each of the four models. Is one model more appealing to members of the group than others?

9. Ask participants to create a draft principal–coach memorandum of understanding (MOU). Be sure to include the coaching expectations, commitments, and assignments you want your coaches to fulfill. Also include the expectations and commitments the coaches can count on from principal leaders. Discuss the benefits of using the MOU.

10. Provide copies of the article "Seventeen Reasons Why Football is Better than High School" (Childress, 1998). Read the article and discuss ways to include the article in your principal preparation plans.

11. Read the scenario below describing Making Strides School District's efforts to implement a change initiative. Discuss the questions that follow.

The Scenario

As is probably true in most school districts, school leaders in the Making Strides School District are encouraged to engage and support teachers in professional learning communities (PLCs) as a protocol for job-embedded professional development. District leaders introduced the PLC concept to principals, assistant principals, and district-level supervisors more than a decade ago as part of their leadership development plan. Following initial professional learning sessions, administrators eagerly took their newly acquired understanding of professional learning communities back to their schools to share with teachers. With time, practice, and ongoing support, some schools solidly embraced the PLC concept and experienced their school cultures evolving into a true community of lifelong learners. However, not all schools were able to build the momentum required to sustain the district's change initiative.

Continual reinforcement and modeling gave principals the necessary support and encouragement to help them develop their understanding and practice of PLCs. Nonetheless, growth and personnel changes led the Making Strides School District to provide additional instruction in professional learning community concepts to school leaders. The plan this time was to make sure the session did not begin with answers—it had to begin with questions. Questions like, "What would it be like if your schools flourished around adult and student learning that was intentional?" Administrators were asked to envision such a school—to imagine what it would look like, what it would sound like, what it would feel like to work and learn in such a setting. During this leadership academy, administrators were given the opportunity to collaborate in their own PLCs, to share best practices, triumphs, and challenges. Before the conclusion of the academy, every school administrator developed an action plan for implementing (or in some cases, strengthening) professional learning communities.

Fast-forward 3 years. Some schools in the Making Strides School District solidly embraced the PLC concept and experienced their school cultures evolving into a true community of lifelong learners. *However, just as before, not all schools were able to build the momentum required to sustain the district's change initiative.*

Questions for Reflection and Discussion

In this scenario, Making Strides School District was unable to generate the required collective capacity to systemically integrate a new professional development model. Even though all principals received ongoing learning opportunities and support for building collaborative school cultures with professional learning communities, the desired change was not developed and sustained in all schools.

- What other measures could district leaders in the Making Strides School District have taken to help schools implement and sustain the PLC model?
- When (if ever) should change be mandated rather than encouraged? What are the benefits and drawbacks of either approach?
- Think of a time when you needed to build collective capacity. How did you go about doing so? How successful were your efforts?
- If you were charged with introducing a new program to your school or district with the expectation for full implementation, what steps would you take to facilitate the change?

Chapter 6 *Anchors Aweigh: Preparing Coaches Through Preservice Instruction*

The Music: "Anchors Aweigh" by Zimmerman (1906)

The Metaphor: For thousands of years, anchors have been used to prevent ships from freely drifting. Whether preparing for rest or bracing for a storm, able-bodied seamen drop anchor to secure their vessel. When the ship's crew is ready to continue their voyage, they must weigh, or hoist, the anchor. This action frees the ship to move. Newly hired coaches present themselves anchored to their roles as classroom teachers. We assist them in weighing anchor—freeing them to assume a new leadership role—through a variety of preservice learning opportunities aimed at aligning coaching activities with school and district goals.

Suggested Activities

1. The opening quote for Chapter 2, attributed to Antoine de Saint-Exupery, cautions us to pay attention to the big picture. Often, newly hired coaches enter their roles with vision limited to their classrooms or schools. With participants, identify the necessary steps to help expand your coaches' vision so they *long for the immensity of the sea.*

2. Consider the size of your district. Is your district so large that some of your new coaches will have never visited other schools or communities within your boundaries? Perhaps you have a small district in which "everybody knows your name." Who in your district is best equipped to provide a detail of school and community demographics, historical data, and interesting facts? Decide if taking time to build understanding and appreciation for the district as a single, unified community will have a positive, long-term impact if included in your preservice learning plans.

3. Several suggested readings to aid in developing a clear understanding of coaching are listed below. Choose one of the readings to complete as an in-depth, self-guided, or facilitated study. Another option is to assign different readings to each member of your group and ask them to present a summary at your next meeting. Prior to their start date, newly hired coaches may be required to read one or more of the books you selected.

Suggested Reading:

Barkley, S. G. (2010). *Quality teaching in a culture of coaching.* Lanham, MD: Rowman & Littlefield Education.

Costa, A. L., & Garmston, R. J. (2002). *Cognitive coaching: A foundation for renaissance schools.* Norwood, MA: Christopher-Gordon.

Killion, J., & Harrison, C. (2006). *Taking the lead: New roles for teachers and school-based coaches.* Oxford, OH: National Staff Development Council.

Knight, J. (2007). *Instructional coaching: A partnership approach to improving instruction.* Thousand Oaks, CA: Corwin.

Knight, J. (2009). *Coaching: Approaches and perspectives.* Thousand Oaks, CA: Corwin.

4. Holonomy may be a new concept for some members of your team. Discuss holonomy, including the idea of both vertical and horizontal holonomy. Identify strategies for increasing your new coaches' sense and awareness of holonomy.

According to Costa and Garmston (2002),

All beings exist within holonomous systems. That is, each person is part of several greater systems (e.g., families, teams, schools) yet maintains a unique identity and palette of choices, both as an independent agent, and a member of a group. Each system influences the individual, and, to a lesser degree, the individual influences the system. (p. 18)

As described in Chapter 6,

The individual coach (part) and his role in the coaching program (whole) represent horizontal holonomy. The individual coach (part) and his role in the school or district (whole) represent vertical holonomy. Coaches must have a clear understanding of their responsibilities to themselves, the coaching program, their schools, and school districts.

5. Lead your group in a discussion using the following questions:
   - What are the specific knowledge and skill sets we want our coaches to deepen and refine?
   - Who are the experts in our organization who will be responsible for leading professional learning activities during the preservice period?
   - What district and/or school goals or initiatives do we want to address during preservice learning?
   - How much time should we allot for implementing our preservice learning plan?
   - How far in advance of the coaches' first day in their schools can we start preservice learning activities?
   - What resources are available to us to implement our plan effectively?

6. Coaches wear many different hats, so at any given time, a coach is a resource provider, data coach, curriculum specialist, instructional specialist, classroom supporter, mentor, learning facilitator, school leader, catalyst for change, and learner (Killion & Harrison, 2006). Create a sample preservice learning agenda that addresses each of the roles you expect your coaches to play. You may wish to create actual hats as visual reminders of which learning activities are supporting which role.

7. Brainstorm the initiatives instructional coaches could help advance in your district. Identify the types of learning opportunities new coaches will need to elevate their level of expertise in these initiatives and increase their opportunities for success.

Chapter 7 *All Hands on Deck: Preparing the Teachers and Staff*

The Music: "Sailing" by Christopher Cross (1979)

The Metaphor: The first time I went sailing on a friend's sailboat, I envisioned myself relaxing like the song by Christopher Cross suggested. I was wrong. Within moments, I discovered that I was supposed to be *doing something* with a rope every minute. "Sailing" sounds very tranquil, but whether you are on a small private yacht or a merchant marine ship, it is actually a lot of work that must be done quickly and simultaneously. When the captain and crew have been chosen and trained and you are ready to finally sail, you need to make sure that everyone—all hands—is ready for the venture. On a large ship the *boatswain* (or bo'sun) historically was the person to call the crew on deck with the phrase "all hands on deck" or "all hands to sail." In your organization, you no doubt have a boatswain (and it might be you!) who is responsible for making sure the work gets done and, at times, for calling *everyone* to work. When that time comes, the boatswain must make sure that all the hands understand their roles and are ready to do their part. As the deck crew's foreman, the boatswain plans the daily work and assignments of the crew, and he or she must have a variety of sailing skills, including handling a variety of emergencies and communicating well with crew of diverse backgrounds and skill sets.

Suggested Activities

1. Share the sailing metaphor or a story of your own experience with sailing. Generate a group discussion to identify the boatswain in

your organization—the key person who knows the ropes and can call all hands to pull the coach and school together.

2. Think about the cultural "lay of the land" in the schools in your district. Are all schools equally prepared to embrace an instructional coaching initiative? Are there schools that have well-established collaborative cultures that could serve as model schools in your district? Are there schools that have attempted to grow a collaborative culture but lack the day-to-day nourishment that an in-house instructional coach can provide? Are there schools in your district that are in more critical need of a change initiative? Discuss how you meet the diverse needs in your district while fostering collaborative cultures for all.

3. Discuss the benefits of having the coach work with teacher leaders in the school before being assigned to work with teachers in need of improvement. What alternate approach might work best in your district?

4. Consider your school or district. What entrenched programs or job positions might feel marginalized by a new coaching program? What steps can you take to keep this from happening?

5. According to Gladwell (2002), three types of people can impact the success of a new idea. *Mavens* are collectors of knowledge and want to review the research and data before forming an opinion. *Connectors* have wide networks and are on friendly terms with most everyone. *Salesmen* (or *persuaders,* in educational terms) are masters of connecting with people on an emotional level and drawing them into their own emotions. Identify the mavens, connectors, and persuaders in your organization. How can you leverage their strengths to champion your coaching initiative?

6. Brainstorm a sticky story about collegiality. Set a timer for 5 minutes and write down all the qualities of coaching you can think of that you would like to express to a school faculty. Then, as a group, share stories of times in your life when a coach helped you or would have helped you by exhibiting those qualities. After discussion, independently write down an outline of your story, being sure to keep it brief and interesting!

7. *Pushback* is a term that describes resistance to a new idea or initiative. In your group, role play several situations in which one person plays the role of the new coach and one person

plays the role of someone resisting the coach's request to collaborate. With each role-play situation you create, vary the degree of pushback. Debrief the role-play experiences from both roles' perspectives. Following are some sample scenarios to help you get started.

Scenario 1

Coach Role: You are a new coach in a school in which teachers have little experience with collaboration, and trust for any outsider is minimal at best. You have been asked to observe a teacher's classroom to determine the fidelity with which a reading initiative is being implemented.

Teacher Role: You are a reading teacher and grade leader. You have 10 years' experience in this position and school and do not like the new reading initiative your district has rolled out. Your student achievement and progress scores have always been solid, so you have no plans to change what you've always done. Your principal introduced the new instructional coach to the faculty during a recent meeting and announced that he will be coming to classrooms to observe. You have made up your mind that you don't need anyone telling you how to teach reading.

Scenario 2

Coach Role: You have been charged with the responsibility of fostering professional learning communities (PLCs) in your school assignment. After discussing school-improvement goals with the principal, you suggest inviting the English department to form a professional learning community (PLC) for the purpose of examining student data. Your principal loves that idea and tells you to get started right away. You bring up the PLC idea while having lunch with some teachers from the English department.

Teacher Role: You are an English teacher at a local high school. As a department, teachers are frightened and anxious about having student achievement data tied to your performance evaluations. You're having lunch with a colleague when the new instructional coach joins you. Right away, she starts talking about professional learning communities and looking at student data. You bristle at the thought of anyone besides your principal knowing your teacher effectiveness results. Besides that, who has time to meet regularly to look at student data?

Scenario 3

Coach Role: You have been assigned to work in a school in which the principal has clearly communicated that she doesn't need a coach in her building—she needs another administrator. You point out the benefits of coaching and that while your role is designed to support teaching and learning, it will also support the principal in her school-improvement efforts.

Principal Role: Your district has rolled out a new instructional coaching program, and you will have an instructional coach assigned to your school. You know there is room for academic and instructional improvement, but how can that happen when your school has so many disciplinary issues? You don't want or need someone else to supervise if they're not there to help with discipline, bus duty, cafeteria duty, and the like. Get real, people!

8. The authors assert that our goal is not to have a coaching program forever, but to have a healthy professional culture in which the capacity of teachers, leaders, and students is maximized. What does maximum capacity look like for teachers, leaders, and students in your school or district?

9. If you don't know what a coach has to offer, it is difficult to know how to use one! Create a menu of coaching activities (modeling, observation, standards alignment, etc.) from which your staff might choose. If you are especially creative, make it look like a real menu!

10. Create a checklist for the principal. List all the items that must be accounted for before the coach arrives—space, time, coach support, and communication structure.

Chapter 8 *Trimming the Sails: Ongoing Professional Learning and Support*

The Music: "Sailing Ships" by Whitesnake (Cloverdale & Vandenberg, 1989)

The Metaphor: Trimming the sails is all about adjusting the tautness of the sails to the speed and direction of the wind in order to move the ship along at your desired clip, or speed. The sails have to be pulled just tightly enough to catch the wind and move the boat forward. If the sails are pulled too tightly, the boat stalls. If the sails are not pulled tightly enough, they luff (or flap loosely), causing the boat to lose speed and direction. We can apply this concept to our instructional coaching program. Once we release the newly prepared instructional coaches to the open waters of schools and classrooms, we need to constantly trim the sails of learning and support for them—too much support smothers, or stalls their progress, while too little support causes them to flounder about aimlessly. We have to provide coaches with the right balance of ongoing learning and support that allows them to assume their roles with confidence and courage.

Suggested Activities

1. Read the metaphor above and discuss with your group how you can achieve the perfect balance of learning and support for your coaches.

2. Make a list of all your in-house experts and their areas of expertise. Consider your district needs and goals as well as the needs and goals of your coaching program. How can you leverage the collective capacity within your organization to provide a comprehensive, ongoing, and sustained learning plan for your coaches?

3. Map out your ideal comprehensive learning plan to support and sustain your coaches. Create an estimated projected budget for your plan.

4. Who are the experts in your state department of education who might be available to provide professional learning for your coaches? Designate one or two members from your group to contact these people to find out their availability for such a request.

5. If you have a local college or university near your district, have someone from your group contact them for potential collaborative learning opportunities.

6. Research grants or other sources that might offset some of the costs associated with your coaches' learning needs.

Chapter 9 *Mooring the Ship: Avalon or Ithaca?*

The Music: "Sitting on the Dock of the Bay" by Otis Redding (Redding & Cooper, 1968)

The Metaphor: In the legend of King Arthur, Avalon is the mystical place where Arthur received Excalibur and where he returned at the end of his life to return the sword. It is a beautiful place, inhabited by magical women, where "no wind blows and where hail, rain and snow have never been known to fall" (Manguel & Guadalupi, 2000, p. 47). In Celtic mythology, Avalon is like the Garden of Eden—it is a place where you do not have to farm the land. The environment simply provides everything you need to survive.

Ithaca is a real island in the Ionic Sea, in contrast to some of the other locations in Homer's *Odyssey*. Ithaca is the home to which Odysseus returns after his life of adventure sailing around the seas, fighting Cyclopes, and avoiding Lotus Eaters. In contrast to Avalon, things were not going so well in Ithaca when Odysseus returned. While he was away, a band of suitors had arrived to steal away his wife and his wealth. To get back his rightful place in the family, he had to pass a test of skill and strength, woo back his wife, kill the suitors, and hang the treacherous maids. Odysseus was almost killed himself, but the goddess Athena intervened and saved him. In Ithaca, everything does not take care of itself.

Suggested Activities

1. Share the contrasting descriptions of Avalon and Ithaca with group members. Create a T-chart and generate a list of descriptors for what Avalon and Ithaca would look like for a new instructional coaching program. Knowing that everything won't take care of itself as you implement your coaching program, discuss the actions your group should take to avoid the trappings that could result from pie-in-the sky expectations or failure to provide everything the coaching program needs to thrive.

2. The authors state that our goal for instructional coaching should be to create a school culture in which change and continual improvement are the norm and risk-taking is encouraged. Where is your organization in relation to this goal?

3. How do you evaluate other professional development models in place in your district? Are the varying approaches you use getting the same results? Are there any approaches you might consider ending?

4. What is your school or district currently spending for professional development? How does that cost compare to your projected costs for implementing an instructional coaching model?

5. As you prepare to launch your own instructional coaching program, how will you answer the following questions: What is best for the students in our school district? Where will coaches have the greatest impact?

6. Read Brutus's lines from Act 4, scene 3 of Shakespeare's *Julius Caesar*. How does this apply to decisions you might make about expanding, sustaining, changing, or abandoning and reimagining your program? Can you think of another poem, saying, or song that gives you courage as you make the decisions ahead?

There is a tide in the affairs of men.

Which, taken at the flood, leads on to fortune;

Omitted, all the voyage of their life

Is bound in shallows and in miseries.

On such a full sea are we now afloat,

And we must take the current when it serves,

Or lose our ventures.

References for Facilitator's Guide

Apted, M. (Director). (2006). *Amazing grace* [Motion picture]. United States: Samuel Goldwyn Films.

Barkley, S. G. (2010). *Quality teaching in a culture of coaching.* Lanham, MD: Rowman & Litchfield Education.

Buffett, J. (1978). Son of a Son of a Sailor. *Son of a Son of a Sailor* [LP]. ABC Dunhill/MCA.

Buxbaum, J. (Creator). (1958–1961). *Sea Hunt* [Television series]. Los Angeles: United Artists Television.

Childress, H. (1998). Seventeen reasons why football is better than high school. *The Phi Delta Kappan, 79*(8), 616–619.

Cloverdale, D., & Vandenberg, A., songwriters. (1989). Sailing Ships [Recorded by WhiteSnake] On *Slip of the Tongue* [LP]. New York: Geffen Records.

Collins, J. (2001). *Good to great: Why some companies make the leap—and others don't.* New York: Harper Business.

Costa, A. L., & Garmston, R. J. (2002). *Cognitive coaching: A foundation for renaissance schools.* Norwood, MA: Christopher-Gordon.

Cross, C. (1979). Sailing. On *Christopher Cross* [LP]. Burbank, CA: Warner Bros. Records.

Dylan, B. (1962). Blowin' in the wind. On *The Freewheelin' Bob Dylan* [LP]. New York: Columbia (1963).

Fullan, M. (2008). *The six secrets of change: What the best leaders do to help their organizations survive and thrive.* San Francisco: Jossey-Bass.

Fullan, M. (2010). *Motion leadership: The skinny on becoming change savvy.* Thousand Oaks, CA: Corwin.

Gladwell, M. (2002). *The tipping point: How little things can make a big difference.* Boston: Back Bay Books.

Gottschalk, L. M. (n.d.). Retrieved from http://www.gottschalk.fr/Biographie/Biographie-eng.htm

Hague, W. (2007). *William Wilberforce: The life of the great anti-slave trade campaigner.* Orlando, FL: Harcourt.

Heath, C., & Heath, D. (2011). Overcoming resistance to change. *School Administrator, 3*, 28–32.

Hoffman, M. (2009, February 16). If Abraham Lincoln had an iPod. *NPR: National Public Radio: News & Analysis, World, US, Music & Arts: NPR.* Retrieved from http://www.npr.org/2009/02/16/100675699/if-abraham-lincoln-had-an-ipod

Hoey, G. (2010). Simplify. On *Utopia* [MP3]. Salem, NH: Wazoo Music Group.

Killion, J. (2008). Courage, confidence, clarity mark the pathway to change. *Journal of Staff Development, 29*(4), 55–59.

Killion, J. (2009). *Coaches' roles, responsibilities, and reach.* In Knight (Ed.), *Coaching approaches and perspectives* (pp. 7–28). Thousand Oaks, CA: Corwin.

Killion, J., & Harrison, C. (2006). *Taking the lead: New roles for teachers and school-based coaches.* Oxford, OH: NSDC.

Kipling, R. (1996). In S. Stuart (Ed.), *A treasury of poems: A collection of the world's most famous verse.* New York: Galahad Books.

Knight, J. (2005). A primer on instructional coaches. *Principal Leadership, 5*(9), 16–21.

Knight, J. (2007). Five key points to building a coaching program. *Journal of Staff Development, 28*(1), 26–31.

Knight, J. (2009). *Coaching: Approaches and perspectives.* Thousand Oaks, CA: Corwin.

Knight, J. (2011). *Unmistakable impact: A partnership approach for dramatically improving instruction.* Thousand Oaks, CA: Corwin.

Lightfoot, G. (1976). The Wreck of the *Edmond Fitzgerald.* On *Summertime Dream* [LP]. Burbank, CA: Reprise Records.

Manguel, A., & Guadalupi, G. (2000). *The dictionary of imaginary places.* New York: Harcourt Brace.

Maxwell, J. C. (2001). *The 21 irrefutable laws of leadership workbook.* Nashville, TN: Thomas Nelson.

Redding, O., & Cropper, S. (1967). Sitting on the dock of the bay [Recorded by Otis Redding]. On *The Dock of the Bay* [LP]. Burbank, CA: Warner Music Group Volto/Atco (1968).

Scott, S. (2004). *Fierce conversations: Achieving success at work & in life, one conversation at a time.* New York: Berkley Books.

Senge, P. M. (2006). *The fifth discipline: The art and practice of the learning organization.* New York: Doubleday/Currency.

Thoreau, H. (2011). *Walden.* Macon, GA: Mercer University Press.

Wilson, P. (n.d.) Blob Tree. *Wimpy player.* Retrieved from http://pipwilsonbhp.blogspot.com/2004/11/blob-tree_110181146915869209.html

Zimmerman, C. (Composer) (1906). Anchors Aweigh [Recorded by U.S. Navy Band]. On *A Patriotic Salute to the Military Family* [MP3]. Franklin, TN: Altissimo Recordings (2001).

Index

Academic performance, 32–33, 39–40
Achebe, C., 93
Action research, 40
Administrative model:
  coaching assignment, 27
  coaching champion, 25–26, 53
  coaching champion team, 23–28
  coaching program development, 23–28
  coaching program goals, 23, 50–51
  coaching roles, 23, 51
  coaching supervision, 24, 25–26, 52–53
  coaching tenure, 27
  coach selection process, 24, 50–54
  communication plan, 26–27
  district-based coaching, 23–24, 51–52
  district policy, 27–28, 53
  labor agreements, 26
  school assignment, 25, 53
  school-based coaching, 23–24, 51–52
AdvancEd, 19
Amazing Grace (2007), 186
"Anchors Aweigh" (1906), 192
Avalon mythology, 120, 200

Backward mapping:
  principal preparation, 66
  staff preparation, 102–103
Balanced coaching, 58–59
Barkley, S. G., 8

Becker, Ron, 74
Benchmarks:
  coaching program development, 23, 130
  sample planning benchmarks, 130
Blob Tree, 45, 181
"Blowin' in the Wind" (1962), 11, 173
Boatswain, 92, 106, 195
Bottom-up plan, 20–21
Brainstorming:
  coaching program development, 28
  staff preparation, 196
Breakfast of Champions, 86–87
Bridges, Lloyd, 37
Buffett, Jimmy, 181

Center for Comprehensive School Reform and Improvement, 103
Change agent role, 67
Change catalyst role, 10–11, 70, 84–85
Childress, H., 191
China, 2
Classroom supporter role, 10–11, 69, 84–85
Cline, Patsy, 161
Coaching academy partnership, 114–115
Coaching Approaches & Perspectives (Knight), 11
Coaching assignment, 27

Coaching basics, 10–11
Coaching champion:
  administrative model, 25–26, 53
  coach selection process, 53
  mini-champions, 94–96
  principal preparation, 72
  professional learning support,
    113, 115, 116–117, 159
  program development, 25–26
  program maintenance, 125
  See also Preservice instruction
Coaching champion team:
  administrative model, 23–28
  conflict resolution, 28
  developmental responsibilities,
    21–28
  program development, 21–28
  team formation, 21
Coaching deep activities, 36–37
Coaching knowledge/skills,
  80–81
Coaching models:
  content-focused model, 11
  evocative coaching, 11
  peer coaching, 11
  2+2 Performance Appraisal
    Model, 11
Coaching orientation interview, 87
Coaching program actualization, 127
Coaching program assessment:
  academic performance, 32–33,
    39–40
  action research, 40
  assessment purpose, 33
  Blob Tree, 45
  coaching deep activities, 36–37
  coaching goals, 33
  coaching interaction chart,
    138–139
  coaching performance data,
    34–35
  coaching shallow activities,
    36–37
  coaching surveys, 40–41
  collaborative school culture,
    32–33
  data collection, 33–35, 38–43
  data communication, 43–44

data distribution, 44–46
data measures, 36–37
data selection determination,
  38–39
data walks, 44–45
facilitator's guide, 179–181
maintenance measures, 121–122
nautical metaphors, 31–32,
  37–38, 179
observation, 42
organizational challenges,
  37–38
organizational support, 39
peer coaching, 33
personal reflection, 42–43
portfolios, 43, 144
principal evaluation data, 34
principal interviews, 41–42
professional learning community
  (PLC), 33
program evaluation data,
  33–34
program goals, 32–33
qualitative data, 42–43
quantitative data, 39–42
reflection exercise, 35, 43
resources, 133–145
sample coach evaluation
  artifacts, 145
sample coaching presentation
  form, 133
sample coaching purchase request
  form, 135–136
sample e-portfolio directions, 144
sample expected coaching
  focus, 134
sample log and itinerary, 140–141
sample recordkeeping
  procedures, 137
sample records communication,
  142–143
stakeholder perceptual data, 33
student data, 32–33, 39–40
success celebration, 46–47
summary, 47
teacher–coach relationship, 35
videotaping, 42
vision statement alignment, 32–33

Coaching program development:
  administrative model application,
    23–28
  bottom-up plan, 20–21
  brainstorming, 28
  coaching champion team,
    21–28
  conflict resolution, 28
  current program assessment,
    17–19
  decision-making level, 20–21
  facilitator's guide, 176–178
  labor division, 21–22
  mission statement alignment,
    15–17, 22
  nautical metaphors, 13, 14,
    19–20, 28, 176
  planning phase, 20–22
  principal participation, 20–21
  professional learning goal, 15–20
  professional learning model,
    17–19
  program flexibility, 22
  progress uncertainty, 14–15
  reflection exercise, 19, 21, 29
  research data, 22
  resources, 128–132
  sample book review chart,
    128–129
  sample goals form, 131–132
  sample planning benchmarks, 130
  stakeholder values, 16–17
  summary, 28–29
  top-down plan, 20–21
  vision statement alignment,
    15–17, 19–20, 22
Coaching program goals:
  administrative model,
    23, 50–51
  coach selection process, 50–51
  program assessment, 32–33
  program development, 23
  sample goals form, 131–132
Coaching program implementation:
  change initiative, 4–6
  coaching basics, 10–11
  coaching models, 11
  coaching roles, 10–11

collaborative school culture, 5
defined, 11
directional goals, 6–8
facilitator's guide, 173–176
implementation challenges,
    3–4, 105–106
literature review, 10–11
maximum capacity, 2–3
mission statement alignment, 7
motivational benefits, 8
nautical metaphors, 2,
    4–11, 173
organizational structure, 9–10
professional learning community
    (PLC), 3
professional learning goal,
    3, 6–7
research overview, 9–10
teacher autonomy, 5
vision statement alignment, 7
Coaching program maintenance:
  actualization process, 127
  coaching champion, 125
  coaching proposal model, 126
  coaching rotation model,
    126–127
  coaching tenure, 126
  facilitator's guide, 200–201
  job-embedded coaching model, 124
  maximum capacity development,
    124–127
  nautical metaphors, 119–121, 200
  part-time coaching model,
    125–126
  peer coaching, 122–123, 125
  professional learning community
    (PLC), 122, 123, 124–125
  program assessment, 121–122
  program elimination, 123–124
  program expansion, 122–123
  program readjustments, 127
  school assignment, 125
  sustainability measures, 123–124
  teaching sabbatical, 126
  vision statement alignment,
    123–124
Coaching program terminology, 82–83
Coaching proposal model, 126

Coaching qualities:
  balanced coaching, 58–59
  coach selection process, 54–62
  courageous coaching, 55–56
  imperative qualities of coaches
    (IQCs), 54
  masterful teacher, 56–58
  person of excellence, 60–62
  treasured coaching, 59–60
  visionary coaching, 55
Coaching roles:
  administrative model, 23, 51
  change catalyst role, 10–11,
    70, 84–85
  classroom supporter role, 10–11,
    69, 84–85
  coach selection process, 51
  curriculum specialist role, 10–11,
    69, 84–85
  data coach role, 10–11, 69, 84–85
  instructional specialist role,
    10–11, 69, 84–85
  learner role, 10–11, 70, 84–85
  learning facilitator role, 10–11,
    69–70, 84–85
  mentor role, 10–11, 70, 84–85
  preservice instruction, 84–85
  principal preparation, 68–70
  program development, 23
  program implementation, 10–11
  resource provider role, 10–11,
    69, 84–85
  school leader role, 10–11, 60,
    84–85
Coaching rotation model, 126–127
Coaching shallow activities, 36–37
Coaching supervision:
  administrative model, 24, 25–26,
    52–53
  coach selection process, 52–53
  district-based coaching, 24, 25–26
  program development, 24, 25–26
  school-based coaching, 24, 25–26
  See also Coaching champion
Coaching surveys, 40–41
Coaching tenure:
  administrative model, 27
  program maintenance, 126

Coach selection process:
  administrative model application,
    24, 50–54
  balanced coaching, 58–59
  coaching qualities, 54–62
  courageous coaching, 55–56
  district-based coaching, 24
  employer references, 59–60
  facilitator's guide, 181–187
  interview questions, 55, 56,
    58, 59, 60, 62
  Level 5 leader, 61
  masterful teacher, 56–58
  nautical metaphors, 49–50,
    58, 181–182
  person of excellence, 60–62
  reflection exercise, 54, 62
  resources, 146–153
  sample content-specific job
    description, 146–147
  sample interview rubric,
    151–153
  sample reference form, 148–150
  school-based coaching, 24
  summary, 63
  treasured coaching, 59–60
  visionary coaching, 55
Collaborative school culture:
  coaching program assessment,
    32–33
  coaching program
    implementation, 5
Collegiality, 101–103
Collins, J. C., 25, 49–50,
    54, 115, 182
Communication models:
  full communication, 72, 190
  positive reinforcement, 72, 190
  principal preparation, 72–73, 190
  silent mentor, 72, 190
  two-way, 72, 190
Communication plan, 26–27
Community relationships:
  guided tours, 83
  preservice instruction, 83
Conferences, 113–114
Conflict resolution, 28
Connectors, 94–96, 196

Consultants, 111–112
Content-focused coaching
   model, 11
Courageous coaching, 55–56
"Crazy" (1961), 161
Cross, Christopher, 195
Cultural environment. *See*
   School culture
Curriculum specialist role,
   10–11, 69, 84–85

Data coach role, 10–11, 69, 84–85
Davis, B. M., 129
Decision-making level, 20–21
Differentiated Coaching (Kise), 129
*Differentiating Instruction in a Whole
   Group Setting* (Pavelka), 129
District-based coaching:
   administrative model, 23–24,
      51–52
   coaching program development,
      23–24
   coaching supervision, 24, 25–26
   coach selection process,
      24, 51–52
   school assignment, 24
   See also School-based coaching
District policy:
   administrative model, 27–28, 53
   coaching program development,
      27–28
   coach selection process, 53
   labor agreements, 26
Dylan, Bob, 11, 173

Edmund Fitzgerald, 179
Employer references, 59–60
Evocative coaching model, 11

Facilitator's guide:
   coach selection process,
      181–187
   content organization, 171–172
   preservice instruction, 192–195
   principal preparation, 188–192
   professional learning support,
      198–199
   program assessment, 179–181

program development, 176–178
program implementation,
   173–176
program maintenance,
   200–201
staff preparation, 195–198
Feeder schools, 24
Fierce Conversations (Scott),
   44, 180
Finland, 2
Flattening world, 2
Friday Focus, 110–111, 165–166
Fullan, M., 67
Full communication model,
   72, 190

Gladwell, M., 94–96, 115
Globalization, 2
Good to Great (Collins), 25, 49–50,
   54, 115, 182
Gottschalk, Louis, 188
Gradual release model, 69
Great Britain, 179

Harrison, C., 189
Heath, C., 5–6
Heath, D., 5–6
Henry V (Shakespeare), 99–100
Hiring process. *See* Coach selection
   process
Hoey, Gary, 176
Hoffman, Miles, 188
Holonomy:
   horizontal holonomy, 85
   preservice instruction, 85
   vertical holonomy, 85
   Homer, 4–5, 60–61, 120, 200
Horizontal holonomy, 85
*How to Coach Teachers Who Don't Think
   Like You* (Davis), 129

If (Kipling), 186–187
"Imagine" (1971), 162
India, 2
Instructional Coaching (Knight),
   8, 129
Instructional specialist role,
   10–11, 69, 84–85

Interactive Think-Aloud Lessons
(Oczukus), 129
International Model
Schools Conference
(Washington, D.C.), 116
Internet resources:
AdvancEd, 19
Blob Tree, 181
Gottschalk, Louis, 188
Learning Forward, 18
YouTube, 180
See also Resources
Ithaca, 120, 200

Job-embedded coaching model, 124

Killion, J., 189
Kipling, R., 186–187
Kise, J. A. G., 129
Knight, J., 8, 11, 129

Labor agreements, 26
Labor division, 21–22
Law of the Few:
connectors, 94–96, 196
mavens, 94–96, 196
salesmen, 94–96, 196
staff preparation,
94–96, 196
Leading in a Culture of Change
(Fullan), 67
Learner role, 10–11, 70, 84–85
Learning facilitator role, 10–11,
69–70, 84–85
Learning Forward, 6–7, 17–18
Lennon, John, 162
Lightfoot, Gordon, 179
Literacy Coaching (Moxley and
Taylor), 129
Literature review:
coaching program development,
128–129
coaching program implementation,
10–11
sample book review chart,
128–129
Longitude Act of 1714
(Great Britain), 179

Marklein, Karen, 75
Masterful teacher, 56–58
Mavens, 94–96, 196
Maximum capacity:
program implementation, 2–3
program maintenance, 124–127
Meetings, 110–111
Memorandum of understanding
(MOU), 74, 190
Mentor role, 10–11, 70, 84–85
Mission statement:
model illustration, 16f
program development,
15–17, 22
program implementation, 7
Morning Edition, 188
Motivation:
program implementation, 8
staff preparation, 96–97
Moxley, D., 129

National Public Radio (NPR), 188
National Staff Development Council.
See Learning Forward
Nation at Risk (1983), 2
Nautical metaphors:
all hands on deck, 91–92, 195
anchors aweigh, 79, 80, 88,
192–193
boarding the ship, 4–6
bon voyage, 111
coach selection process, 49–50, 58,
181–182
consulting the compass, 6–8,
111, 161
dead reckoning, 13, 14,
19–20, 176
feeling the wind in your hair, 8
following North stars, 10–11
getting their sea legs, 58
leadership, 65–66, 188
mooring the ship, 119–121, 200
perfect storm, 2, 106, 173
preservice instruction, 79, 80, 88,
192–193
prevailing winds, 1–4, 173
principal preparation,
65–66, 188

professional learning support,
    109, 110, 198–199
program assessment, 31–32,
    37–38, 179
program development, 13, 14,
    19–20, 28, 176
program implementation,
    2, 4–11, 173
program maintenance,
    119–121, 200
ready, set, sail, 49–50,
    181–182
sailing with the current, 9–10
shipwrecks, 31–32
sounding the depths, 31–32,
    179–181
squalls, 28
staff preparation, 91–92, 105–106, 195
trimming the sails, 109, 110,
    198–199
No Child Left Behind Act (2001),
    2, 123

Observation, 42
O Captain! My Captain!
    (Whitman), 188
Oczukus, L., 129
Odyssey (Homer), 4–5, 60–61,
    120, 200
Outliers (Gladwell), 115

Part-time coaching model, 125–126
Pavelka, P., 129
Peer coaching:
    principal preparation, 74–75
    program assessment, 33
    program maintenance,
        122–123, 125
    2+2 Performance Appraisal
        Model, 11
Personal reflection, 42–43
Person of excellence, 60–62
Pink, D., 115
Portfolios:
    program assessment, 43, 144
    sample e-portfolio
        directions, 144
Positive reinforcement communication
    model, 72, 190

Preservice instruction:
    Breakfast of Champions,
        86–87
    coaching knowledge/skills,
        80–81
    coaching program terminology,
        82–83
    coaching roles, 84–85
    community guides, 83
    community knowledge, 83
    facilitator's guide, 192–195
    holonomy, 85
    nautical metaphors, 79, 80,
        88, 192–193
    orientation interview, 87
    plan development, 81–82
    principal role, 86–88
    reflection exercise, 81, 86
    resources, 155
    sample welcome letter to newly
        hired coaches, 155
    vision statement alignment, 82
Principal preparation:
    backward design, 66
    change agent role, 67
    coaching champion role, 72
    coaching roles, 68–70
    communication models,
        72–73, 190
    facilitator's guide, 188–192
    instructional coaching value, 68
    memorandum of understanding
        (MOU), 74, 190
    nautical metaphors, 65–66, 188
    peer coaching, 74–75
    principal role, 70–71
    reflection exercise, 70, 73,
        74, 76
    resources, 154
    sample plan, 75–76
    summary, 76
    See also Staff preparation
Principal role:
    assessment interviews, 41–42
    evaluation data, 34
    orientation interview, 87
    preservice instruction, 86–88
    program assessment, 34, 41–42
    program development, 20–21

Professional learning community
(PLC):
program assessment, 33
program implementation, 3
program maintenance,
122, 123, 124–125
Professional learning goal:
program development, 15–20
program implementation,
3, 6–7
Professional learning model:
defined, 6, 18
program development, 17–19
Professional learning support:
coaching academy partnership,
114–115
coaching champion, 113, 115,
116–117, 159
conferences, 113–114
consultants, 111–112
Consulting the Compass,
111, 161
facilitator's guide, 198–199
Friday Focus, 110–111, 165–166
meetings, 110–111
nautical metaphors, 109, 110,
198–199
reflection exercise, 111, 112,
115, 117
resources, 156–166
sample coach–coach support, 159
sample consulting-the-compass
activity, 161
sample culture of coaching
activity, 156
sample Friday Focus, 165–166
sample gripes-to-goals activity, 157
sample imagine activity, 162
sample imagine scenarios,
163–164
sample individual reflection, 160
sample peer coaching
assignment, 158
Si C-C meetings, 111
site visits, 114
summary, 117
technology training, 112–113
Project RAISSE, 125
Pushback, 196–197

Qualitative data, 42–43
Quality Teaching in a Culture of Coaching
(Barkley), 8
Quantitative data, 39–42
Quantum Learning, 171

Reading Assistance Initiative for
Secondary School Educators
(RAISSE), 125
Redding, Otis, 200
Resistance, 97, 196–197
Resource provider role,
10–11, 69, 84–85
Resources:
coaching interaction chart,
138–139
coach selection process, 146–153
preservice instruction, 155
principal preparation, 154
professional learning support,
156–166
program assessment, 133–145
program development, 128–132
sample book review chart,
128–129
sample coach–coach support, 159
sample coach evaluation
artifacts, 145
sample coaching presentation
form, 133
sample coaching purchase request
form, 135–136
sample consulting-the-compass
activity, 161
sample content-specific job
description, 146–147
sample culture of coaching
activity, 156
sample e-portfolio directions, 144
sample expected coaching
focus, 134
sample Friday Focus, 165–166
sample goals form, 131–132
sample gripes-to-goals activity, 157
sample imagine activity, 162
sample imagine scenarios, 163–164
sample individual reflection, 160
sample interview rubric, 151–153
sample log and itinerary, 140–141

sample orientation for instructional coaching, 154
sample peer coaching assignment, 158
sample planning benchmarks, 130
sample recordkeeping procedures, 137
sample records communication, 142–143
sample reference form, 148–150
sample welcome letter to newly hired coaches, 155
See also Internet resources

"Sailing" (1979), 195
"Sailing Ships" (1989), 198
Salesmen, 94–96, 196
Sample forms. *See* Resources
School assignment:
    administrative model, 25, 53
    coaching program development, 25
    coaching program maintenance, 125
    coach selection process, 53
    See also District-based coaching; School-based coaching
School-based coaching:
    administrative model, 23–24, 51–52
    coaching program development, 23–24
    coaching supervision, 24, 25–26
    coach selection process, 24, 51–52
    school assignment, 24
    See also District-based coaching
School culture:
    coaching program assessment, 32–33
    collaboration, 5, 32–33
    collegiality, 101–103
    cultural environment, 92–93
    environmental context, 103–105
    staff preparation, 92–93, 101–106
School leader role, 10–11, 69, 84–85
School mission. *See* Mission statement
School vision. *See* Vision statement
Scott, S., 44, 180
Sea Hunt, 37, 180
Seaman's Act (1915), 181
"Seventeen Reasons Why Football is Better than High School" (Childress), 191

Shakespeare, W., 99–100
Si C-C meetings, 111
Silent mentor communication model, 72, 190
"Simplify" (2010), 176
Singapore, 2
Site visits, 114
"Sitting on the Dock of the Bay" (1968), 200
Sociocultural learning theory, 2–3
"Son of a Son of a Sailor" (1978), 181
South Korea, 2
Staff preparation:
    backward mapping, 101
    cultural collegiality, 101–103
    cultural environment, 92–93
    facilitator's guide, 195–198
    implementation challenges, 105–106
    Law of the Few, 94–96, 196
    message clarification, 97
    mini-champions, 94–96
    motivational factors, 96–97
    nautical metaphors, 91–92, 106, 195
    program resistance, 97, 196–197
    pushback, 196–197
    reflection exercise, 94, 96
    school environment, 103–105
    sticky ideas, 97, 98, 102, 196
    storytelling, 99–100
    summary, 106–107
    teacher leaders, 93–94
    Tiger Woods syndrome, 98
    transactive memory, 101
    vision statement alignment, 96–97
    vital behaviors, 103
    See also Principal preparation
Stakeholders:
    program assessment, 33
    program development, 16–17
Standards for Professional Learning (Learning Forward), 17–18
Sticky ideas, 97, 98, 102, 196
Storytelling, 99–100
Student data, 32–33, 39–40
Sullivan, Danny, 74–75
Switch (Heath and Heath), 5–6

Taking the Lead (Killion and Harrison), 189
Taylor, R., 129
Teacher autonomy, 5
Teacher–coach relationship, 35
Teacher leaders, 93–94
Teacher preparation. *See* Staff preparation
Teaching sabbatical, 126
Technology training, 112–113
Things Fall Apart (Achebe), 93
Thoreau, H. D., 176
Tiger Woods syndrome, 98
Tipping Point, The (Gladwell), 94–96
Top-down plan, 20–21
Transactive memory, 101
Treasured coaching, 59–60
Turner, Andrew, 74
Turn to Your Neighbor activity, 173
2+2 Performance Appraisal Model, 11
Two-way communication model, 72, 190

"Union, The" (1862), 188
Unmistakable Impact (Knight), 11
U.S. Department of Education, 3

Vertical holonomy, 85
Videotaping, 42
Visionary coaching, 55
Vision statement:
    model illustration, 16f
    preservice instruction, 82
    program assessment, 32–33
    program development, 15–17, 19–20, 22
    program implementation, 7
    program maintenance, 123–124
    staff preparation, 96–97
Vital behaviors, 103

Walden (Thoreau), 176
Walton High School (Marietta, Georgia), 122–123
Whitesnake, 198
Whitman, W., 188
Whole New Mind, A (Pink), 115
Wilberforce, William, 186
Wilson, Pip, 45, 181
Woods, Tiger, 98
"Wreck of the *Edmund Fitzgerald*, The" (1976), 179

YouTube, 180

Zimmerman, C., 192

CORWIN
A SAGE Company

The Corwin logo—a raven striding across an open book—represents the union of courage and learning. Corwin is committed to improving education for all learners by publishing books and other professional development resources for those serving the field of PreK–12 education. By providing practical, hands-on materials, Corwin continues to carry out the promise of its motto: **"Helping Educators Do Their Work Better."**